TWO ELEPHANTS IN THE ROOM
EVOLVING CHRISTIANITY AND LEADERSHIP

JOHN BODYCOMB

First published in Australia in 2018
by Spectrum Publications Pty Ltd
a: PO Box 75, Richmond, Victoria, Australia 3121
t: (+61) 1300 540 736
f: (+61) 1300 540 737
e: spectrum@spectrumpublications.com.au
w: www.spectrumpublications.com.au
for John Bodycomb

© 2018 John Bodycomb
All rights reserved.
No part of this publication may be reproduced
in any manner without prior written permission of the publisher.
Cover Design: Tregraphic
Typesetting by Spectrum Publications Pty Ltd
Typeface: Georgia & Avenir

ISBN 978-0-86786-009-2

 A catalogue record for this book is available from the National Library of Australia

CONTENTS

Preface	iv
Introduction	vii
Part I: Is *homo religiosus* becoming extinct?	
CH. 1 – OVERVIEW: RELIGION AND NON-RELIGION	1
CH. 2 – THE EARLIEST IMPULSE TOWARD 'RELIGION'	15
CH. 3 – WHEN RELIGION IS NO LONGER SEEN AS ESSENTIAL	25
Part II: So, what is happening and why?	
CH. 4 – THE FORBIDDING FUTURE	42
CH. 5 – EVOLVING ORGANISM – PANORAMIC VIEW	50
CH. 6 – EVOLVING ORGANISM – PROXIMATE VIEW	61
CH. 7 – RESPONSES MALADAPTIVE AND ADAPTIVE	74
Part III: The Future for Religious Leadership	
CH. 8 – THE EMERGING RELIGIOUS PROFESSIONAL	84
CH. 9 – WILL WE HAVE ANY RECRUITS?	102
CH. 10 – WHAT SHALL WE DO WITH THEM?	110
Coda	**117**
Bibliography	**120**

PREFACE

Drafting **Two Elephants** in the winter of 2014, I wrote "What makes a man of 83 decide on his early morning walk that he may have one more book in him – waiting to be written? On the face of it, such a notion can sound like delusion if not dementia, or at the very least, like self-display!"

I am willing to consider such allegations, all of which could have a basis in fact. However, something else was driving this exercise. It is 'elephants in the room' – pachyderms in the parlour! Despite its frequently good quality, too much of today's writing in religious matters looks to be evasive of uncomfortable truths. Official rhetoric from ecclesiastical boffins and boards is often larded with fallacies, fantasies and fibs, in a concerted effort to avoid upsetting anyone.

Hence the choice of title: "Two Elephants in the Room". One of these pesky pachyderms is the future of organised religion in Western society. The other is the future of religious professionals; 'god-botherers' as they are affectionately known in some quarters. In a word, will Western society continue to need clergy and if so, why? What will they be doing?

It was actually the latter issue that was haunting me at the time. There has been much written on the future of organised religion, but a good deal less on what I call 'RELPROS' – religious professionals. Along with the shaking of the foundations (to pinch Paul Tillich's book title), from the 1950s onward came the spooking of the functionaries as they began facing questions hitherto under the rug.

My contemporaries and I, in college/seminary during the early 50s, were aware of these and tussled with them as best we could. That they were not about to go away was clearly apparent to us when tortured colleagues began to spill the beans. At a clergy conference in 1957, walking along that mountain road lit by a crescent moon, a man much senior to me said, "John, what are you planning to say about the resurrection on Easter Day? I can't believe that stuff."

Over more than sixty years there have been thousands of one-on-one chats with religious professionals of every Christian persuasion where problems with structures of belief have come to the fore. This is, in fact, the single major cause of 'relpros' unravelling. Why, then, is it not more readily aired? Six reasons:

- The enormity of the issues generates 'avoidance' mechanisms
- The desire to stay within one's network precludes disclosures
- Most need to locate causes of problems outside themselves
- The notion of 'apostasy' can have heavy moral connotations
- To concede unbelief says personal and professional life have been grounded on mistaken premises
- Belief and identity are so closely intertwined that collapse of one can make collapse of the other imminent

(John Bodycomb. Why RELPROS Unravel)

The truth of the matter is that few if any occupations have a bigger casualty rate than religious professionals. We have scant information of an exact nature on Australia, exit from the forms of paid ministry being often camouflaged under a term like 'otherwise employed'. But we do have graphic data from what is arguably still the most 'religious' of Western nations – USA.

Tanner *et al*, in 'Forced Termination of American Clergy', find exit at some point in the work of ministry to be around 25 percent in a number of US denominations. The figure is highest in Assemblies of God, at 41 percent. They also point out that in any given year 20,000 ministers in the US leave their profession permanently! The quarter who leave have a mix of psychologically deleterious effects, and may carry some bruising to their subsequent employment.

(Marcus Tanner et al. "Forced Termination of American Clergy")

Had it been thought that the 1968 landmark research of Jud and Mills in the US might give the system a good shake, this looks to be unlikely.

(Gerald Jud & Edgar Mills. 'Ex-Pastors: why men leave the parish ministry')

Our own Norman Blaikie, a decade or so later, was writing about the widespread discomfiture of religious professionals, but he scarcely raised an eyebrow in the halls of theological education.

(Norman Blaikie. 'The Plight of the Australian Clergy')

That, of course, was my own experience over a decade working in theological education. Hence my fear that we were programming men and women for failure – according to a model that belonged to another era.

It was this issue that underlay **Two Elephants** in the first instance, but then I realised that it was fatuous to pursue this without setting it squarely in the context of what was happening to organised religion in Western societies. Defining the profession of 'ministry' according to a set of unquestioned assumptions based on our traditional theology of 'Church, Ministry & Sacraments', plus a mix of doctrines about 'Ordination', could no longer be defended.

It has been a wild ride, and I am deeply indebted to many. As always I have had some wonderful critics ready to speak the truth in love! Most especially I would thank my dear wife Lorraine Parkinson for her encouragement, candid comments and wise suggestions. I thank also my good friend Peter Rohr, manager of Spectrum Publications, for risking his reputation and that of the firm once again!

JOHN BODYCOMB – August 2018

INTRODUCTION

BUSY DOING NOTHING

In the movie *A Connecticut Yankee in King Arthur's Court*, Bing Crosby sings with William Bendix and Sir Cedric Hardwicke, "We're busy doing nothing, working the whole day through, trying to find lots of things not to do ..." We are quite adept at this in the church, which includes nonsensical research projects that yield nonsensical results and nonsensical reports. These days it is hardly surprising that so many should be sceptical about so-called research.

Do you ever have one of those maddening 'phone calls at meal time that start, "Allo. Is that John?" "Who is calling?" "This is International Surveys Limited." "You're selling something." "Oh, no, John. This is a genuine offer." "Of what?" "A once-in-a-lifetime offer to specially chosen people like you. May I just ask you a few questions?" CLUNK! (That is the sound of my phone being slammed down on its mounting)

Calls like this, which are either market research or more often straight-out selling, get survey research a bad name. But some is genuine, and it gets someone a university degree or even publication in some journal, while adding virtually nothing to the pool of human knowledge. Never mind; someone looks busy!

During my initial education for ministry, several summers went on factory labouring work, to accumulate funds for the ensuing year. One day in a food processing plant, while I was idly waiting for a stalled machine to re-start, the shop steward raced up to me and barked, "Boss has his eye on you. For krissake (or something like that) grab a broom and start sweeping." I looked around, fortunately found one and set about obeying orders. It mattered not that the floor was almost clean and that having swept a small amount of dirt one way, I then turned around and swept it back. Had to look busy, you see.

Reflecting on that experience 64 years later, I'm reminded of my wife's poster of a kitten – walking back and forth on a computer keyboard. The caption is "If you don't know what you're doing, look busy." She suggests this axiom is sometimes exemplified in churches. In fact, I have an 'icon' of the phenomenon in a little handcrafted wooden device that sits atop my filing cabinet. When the handle is turned, pieces move alternately back and forth in fitting grooves. It is called a "Do Nothing" machine. Looks impressive!

In 2014 the Uniting Church's 'VicTas' Synod announced the high-sounding "Major Strategic Review", and circulated a questionnaire I would have failed outright when I taught sociology. But this created the illusion that something of worth was happening.

I have an unpublished paper in the computer titled "Asking the Wrong Questions". Its uncomplicated thesis is that asking the wrong questions guarantees finding the wrong answers! Naturally, what follows on this is the administering of wrong prescriptions. We need to be asking the right questions. This is what I try to do in the pages that follow. These have been foreshadowed in the Preface, and need not be repeated here.

But there is ...

A HUGE QUESTION COMMONLY AVOIDED

What must be mentioned in this introduction, without which to continue would be fruitless, is the single biggest question that confronts adherents of all 'theistic' religions and, almost equally, the general public in Western societies – whether or not they have any affinity with organised religion. So, what is this question? It is this: In a world where we know we are seven million miles away in space from where we were this time last week, and in a universe nearly fourteen billion years old, what ever do we think we mean by the formula 'G-O-D'?

I was rudely awakened to this forty years ago by my colleague the late Professor Robert Anderson, with whom I was discussing how Jesus had been turned into a deity by the movement that survived him. I had said to Robert that the whispers I heard from candid pewsitters were pointing toward the likely collapse of classical 'christology'. "Oh, nonsense, John!" came back sharply. "That's inevitable and that discussion is over. The real question is what ever we think we mean by 'God'!"

Trying to look busy these past two thousand years, Christianity's manufacturers and distributors of godtalk have delivered a bedazzling conglomerate of beautiful nonsense that few but they and their acolytes have been able to understand. Churches duly lurched unsteadily into the 20th century (not to mention the 21st!) repeating pre-Copernican, mediaeval claptrap about God.

Their nonsense somehow survived the scientific knowledge given us in the 20th century, and continues enshrined in the hymns, prayers and pulpit pronouncements of men and women who should know better. The Bible says it is a terrible thing to fall into the hands of a living God. It is also a terrible thing to be delivering nonsense on the subject of whatever this 'transcendent' Something is.

It would be some thirty years years since I first (and guardedly) used the somewhat facetious term 'cetacean shutterbugs'. I am less guarded these days, as the reader will quickly sense. Such is the privilege (or trap) of getting old. My intent was to show how overrated both 'godtalk' (theology) and its manufacturers and distributors were. It was a plea for humility in our declarations about the Divine, commonly issued with such confidence and pomp!

I used the metaphor of a whale spotting cruise in the Southern Ocean, out to photograph blue whales. At 140 tonnes and more, the blue whale is the largest animal ever, and my fanciful tour party of wealthy whale-spotters had an air of competition about it. When one of these breathtaking creatures surfaced in clear view, all our photographers were clicking away feverishly, duly comparing results and arguing about whose images best captured this leviathan of the deep. Each claimed a better success rate.

In my use of this whale-spotting metaphor, I made the point (hardly necessary), that little static, two-dimensional snaps in no way could ever be said to have captured this huge, dynamic, ever-moving phenomenon. Besides, all of these cetacean shutterbugs brought to the exercise different perspectives, different equipment, different skills. In like manner, it seemed to me that presuming to capture in the word pictures of godtalk (theology) this Ineffable Mystery of whom we dare to speak was a somewhat similar exercise.

Around this time I had been given, by a university student I had helped, a copy of the brilliant work 'Old Turtle', written by Douglas Wood and illustrated by Cheng-Khee Chee. An exquisite yarn equally suited to adults and children, it begins with all the components in creation arguing about God. Not surprisingly, they all make God in their own image, but there is a beautiful outcome. You need to read/hear the story. But in the meantime, consider these words from the New Zealand hymn writer Lois Henderson:

> *O God, beyond our knowledge, time and space,*
> *and yet within each person in this place;*
> *we sing with grateful thanks and heartfelt praise*
> *your love that warms and colours all our days.*
>
> *Around us living things your wonder show;*
> *the birds above, each tree and flower below*
> *of ev'ry colour, fragrance, texture, size,*
> *unveil your lavish love to marv'ling eyes.*

*You feel our deepest sorrow, fears and needs,
transform compassion to creative deeds;*
you gently crumble long held rigid creeds;
replace with unimagined lively seeds.

*You come in thunder, silence, ice and flame;
enrich the poor, make dancers of the lame;
in vain we try to keep you neatly filed;
ruler of realms, yet helpless human child.*

*We cannot comprehend what you have planned,
but trust your wisdom and your gen'rous hand;
may we, with awe and joy, use what you give
that ev'rything on earth may truly live.*

<u>Source:</u> Hope is our Song: New Hymns and Songs from Aotearoa New Zealand, the New Zealand Hymnbook Trust

You gently crumble long held rigid creeds. I love that! But how did I get to be so cynical about godtalk, and about those who engage in it with such conceit? Not just via 'Old Turtle' and Lois Henderson. I guess it has much to do with my induction in 1967, at Boston University, into to the company of sociologists of religion, which was duly followed by a cataclysmic change to my ways of thinking. I came to see all religious life and thought as *ephemeral human artifacts* – subject to the same forces that impinge on everything else we think and make and do.

To put this another way, I stopped thinking that because 'God' was overseeing all this, godtalk therefore had some sort of extra-mundane or supernatural guardianship, guiding hand and protection against all weathers! Now, it just *may* have all of these advantages, and it just *may* be somehow immune to the ravages of time and circumstance (not to mention the limitations of human frailty) – but I'm afraid I don't see the compelling evidence for that claim.

My metaphor of 'cetacean shutterbugs' was duly topped by another and far better metaphor, when our great home-grown theologian Val Webb released a work called *Like Catching Water in a Net* and said:

> "There is a difference between knowing that Something exists (or doesn't) and knowing what it might be (or not be). The former comes through experiences of awe, contact or fear which, on reflection, seem orchestrated from beyond." ('Like Catching Water in a Net', p.2)

So to one of my own favourite stories in the Hebrew scriptures; it's in Exodus 3. Whether or not it is historically verifiable matters not a jot; it is a great yarn with a message for all of us. While minding the flock of his father-in-law Jethro, Moses has a mystical experience of immense power. He encounters a fearful spectacle: a bush that is ablaze – crackling and roaring, yet not consumed by the flames. From within it he seems to hear a Voice, informing him that he is to lead his people out of their slave conditions in Egypt. Moses asks who is speaking to him. The Voice replies in Hebrew *'ehyeh asher ehyeh'*. That means not "I am who I am", as is often thought, but "I will be who I will be!"

Tantalisingly cryptic, mystifying and non-committal when you think about it. Moses hears the Voice saying, "You will *never, never* know my personal name!" I take this to be the definitive statement for all time and all peoples that they will *never* pin down the ineffable mystery to any slick slogan, much less impermeable dogma. To delude oneself that such might be possible is conceit of the *nth* degree.

So, do I believe in God? That is a silly question! I am a 'theist' and unashamedly so. But stop right here! 'G-O-D' is not a name; it is only a noun commonly spelled with a capital letter. It is better understood as a 'formula', like H_2O or CO_2. As a theist I believe that this formula denotes something that is eminently real, just as I believe that H_2O and CO_2 denote something eminently real.

For the sake of clarification, an atheist believes that there is no counterpart in reality for the formula 'G-O-D'; it is a word/term/formula like *qwertyuiop* – the top line of your keyboard. An agnostic believes there is not sufficient evidence to arrive at any conviction. An adiaphorist (from the Greek word for 'indifference') couldn't care less. An increasing number of Westerners may be closer to the last mentioned.

It is not easy to say with accuracy and confidence how many of Earth's people are 'theists'; i.e. confident believers that the formula 'G-O-D' refers to something real. However, using a range of sources and figures currently available, one can say that between 80 and 85 percent of the world's population seem to think there's something.

About seven out of ten of these people would call themselves Christian, Muslim or Hindu of one variety or another. Major 'non-theistic' religions are Chinese, Buddhist and Primal/Indigenous. In other words, one cannot easily say that for the bulk of the world's people "God is dead." On the contrary. Insofar as such a proportion of earth-dwellers are 'theistic' in some form, perhaps some crazy and unworthy ideas about 'G-O-D' deserve to be challenged. This surely is a task facing churches and religious professionals.

WHO (OR WHAT) IS 'G-O-D' FOR ME?

So, who or what is 'G-O-D' for this old unredeemed theist? For me 'G-O-D' is not a personal name. Neither does it refer to a 'being'. It is the formula I use to denote this ineffable Mystery that:

- *IMAGINES the possibility of a universe*
- *INTENDS that the universe should be*
- *INITIATES this universe (the 'Big Bang')*
- *INFORMS it (in continuing release of information)*
- *INFLUENCES it subtly from within*
- *INSPIRES it to be the best that it can be*

In this I am much closer to some of the modern scientists, like Professor Paul Davies, currently at Arizona State University, Director of BEYOND: Center for Fundamental Concepts in Science, and author of more than twenty major works. At the launch in Melbourne of one such, I said to Professor Davies, "Given that 'G-O-D' is a *formula* for something, does it still have some cash value for you?" (My exact words) "Oh, indeed ... but not the way churches talk about it!" (his exact words) It should be apparent from my six verbs starting with 'i', above, that the formula 'G-O-D' is rich with meaning for me also – but not the way churches talk about it. I find much of the churches' godtalk trivialises this Mystery and can sound juvenile.

Sometimes, especially when trying to explain 'G-O-D' to children, I use the metaphor of 'the ocean of being'. I say to them that we live in God, just as fish live in the sea – and that also (in a small way) the sea is in the fish. This way of thinking about 'G-O-D' is called 'panentheism'. I suppose it makes me a 'panentheist'. It is why I have said in other writings that for me 'G-O-D' is:

> *"the surrounding, saturating, sacred presence in whom dwells everything and everyone, who indwells everything and everyone, who envelops and infuses all that is. God is in all and all is in God."*

I have little patience with those who caricature 'theism' as a superstitious belief in some manipulating *and* manipulable entity: the 'straw man' argument. Some of these have invented a new term for themselves. This is the word 'a-theist', which goes with 'a-theism'. It is meant to convey the message that they have ditched the divinity that I and other theists allegedly still believe in! In some quarters it is the great new word; I find it unhelpful. Some of the most voluble give little or no evidence of engaging with scholars in the other great monotheistic faiths, or with philosophers, or with cosmologists. I have been enriched in dialogue with all these, and in consequence remain unabashedly 'theistic' – but the Divinity I worship and to whom I listen for those 'holy whispers' is far, far removed from the Divinity repudiated by my atheist friends and my 'a-theist' friends. This Divinity is the *dianoia kosmou*, or mind of the cosmos. (Refer my book 'No Fixed Address', pp 217ff)

In passing, I am similarly at some distance from the conventional ways of speaking about Jesus. We have not only created an intellectual monstrosity by turning him into a deity, but in so doing have 'de-natured' the most enlightened human being in history. For me Jesus is to the art of living as Einstein is to cosmology. The late Arthur Peacocke (1924-2006), Anglican priest and one time professor of biochemistry at Oxford, saw Jesus as the pinnacle of human evolution, and described him as "the God-informed person *par excellence.*" (Arthur Peacocke, 'Zygon' pp.639-659) I like that.

THE TWO ELEPHANTS

This is not primarily a book about God or about Jesus, much less about my own journey. There is plenty about all three of those matters in my book *No Fixed Address*. However, as a way into *Two Elephants* I have to recall here one personal experience. In 1951 I relinquished my future with a US company in Australia, and told my paternal grandfather that I was entering theological school. "You're mad!" he said. "The church is dying, and you will be out of a job!" I have never been out of work, and the church is not dead – yet. But nonetheless, was my grandfather more farsighted than he knew?

Picking up on his terse rebuke, this work addresses two issues that have exercised me virtually since first entering theological school in 1952: the future of organised religion in Western society, and the future of that profession commonly called 'ordained minister'. These are the two elephants in the room, that my grandfather may have spotted when they were just baby elephants. But baby elephants grow, and in the end cannot be ignored, however hard we may be trying to look away.

Later I shall be inviting my reader to consider religion in general as being rather like some sort of evolving organism, living in a symbiotic relationship with the cultural environment. The main thing is that I will be trying to show that history demonstrates how religion(s) evolve or die.

I have also learned how wretchedly difficult it can be to agree on what we mean by that word 'religion'. I have at times driven people mad with my refusal to get into arguments until there was some agreement on what was meant by words being used. For instance, when I was chaplain at the University of Melbourne, eager-beaver students would inquire if I believed that Jesus was 'the son of God' and/or that he was 'divine'. I would say, "Tell me what you mean by that, and then I can say if I agree with you." Blank looks followed.

The first chapter of *Two Elephants*, 'Religion and Non-religion', deals with this problem of definition, and how we can decide whether people may be more (or less) interested in it. We turn then to looking at the concept of religion as an evolving thing: an organism in the cultural gloop, that changes or dies (to steal the title of a book by John Shelby Spong). In this section we take what I call a 'panoramic view', spanning 6-7 centuries, and then a 'proximate view' – looking at some observable and compelling reasons why religion must change or die!

The last section of *Two Elephants* looks at the religious professional: what he/she may be expected to be and do in the future – and how he/she is to be equipped for this role. Confusion reigns supreme in this matter. Hence the massive numbers of clergy, in all persuasions, registering burn-out, freak-out, drop-out – just wanting to be somewhere else!

The material is presented in a flexible form – such as might have allowed me to deliver it in the form of stand-alone lectures, in part or *in toto* as a series of lectures over weeks, as the substance of an 'intensive' conference or (for those who prefer to take it in via the eye) simply as a published book. In fact, some of it has already been delivered in three states and overseas where my wife Lorraine Parkinson and I have had invitations from those eager to explore new ground. I acknowledge my indebtedness to good people in Western Australia, Queensland and the Northern Territory, as well as in Victoria, and also in New Zealand, whose listening and responses have aided in its fine-tuning.

Two Elephants does not pretend to set down everything I think about evolving Christian thought and leadership. However, it *does* rest on 66 years as a 'participant-observer', counting my initial theological education and subsequent years as a religious professional. It is not intended as the last word on anything. I want to emphasise that, because my own experience is that one discovers something new every single day – if he/she is open to it. Such was the message of *No Fixed Address: Faith as Journey.*

PART I

Is *homo religiosus* becoming extinct?

CHAPTER 1

OVERVIEW: RELIGION AND NON-RELIGION

In 1962 a pious young woman of Irish extraction, born at Wildmoor in Worcestershire, entered upon life with a strict order of religious sisters. After seven years and her dawning awareness that the draconian regime was not where she belonged, Karen Armstrong quit the convent – thereby doing the academic and religious world a massive service. Today she is among the topmost historians of religion, widely recognised for her scholarship and her writing. In the opening of one major work Karen Armstrong declares:

> *My study of the history of religion has revealed that human beings are spiritual animals. Indeed, there is a case for arguing that Homo sapiens is also Homo religiosus.*
>
> ('A History of God', *xix*)

The truth or otherwise in that statement has long exercised me, and took me in 1967 to the USA. The late 60s would have to be among the more turbulent periods in American history, both for the churches and for the larger society. The former (clergy especially) were unsettled by the so-called 'new morality' and 'death of God' movements, and in addition to these the anti-war and civil rights movements were at their height. In 1968 Martin Luther King and Robert Kennedy were assassinated barely two months apart. I was living in the middle of this maelstrom of intellectual and socio-political turmoil.

I had gone to Boston University to study sociology and social ethics. Some thought I had gone there to become a *social worker* – such was the lack of acquaintance with sociology. According to the Macquarie dictionary, sociology is "the science or study of the origin, development, organisation, and functioning of human society; the science of the fundamental laws of human relations, institutions, etc." The pioneer patriarch of the field is generally agreed to be the French philosopher Émile Durkheim (1858-1917).

WHAT IS 'RELIGION'?

A branch of the discipline is the study of religion, which as a socio-cultural phenomenon looks to be nearly as old as *homo sapiens*, as Karen Armstrong suggests. Just as this species of life (homo sapiens) has many sub-species, so it is with the forms of society they have developed – *and* the forms of religion that exist in those societies. My major focus became the sociology of religion, and ultimately, the growth and/or decline of organised religion – as in Western society (especially Australia). But what is **religion**?

When someone describes her grandma to me as very religious, an image comes at once to mind: a little old lady in a shawl, seated in her rocking chair on the verandah and peering intently through fine-rimmed spectacles at the open Bible in her knotty hands – perhaps muttering quietly to herself. "Swotting for her finals" as I once heard her described! This is the image that 'religious' suggests to many.

In Israel it is the image of a man in black (no, not Johnny Cash!) who, with his modestly clad wife and numerous children, keeps himself as far as possible separate from the larger 'secular' society. These so-called 'Haredim' (Ultra-Orthodox) are distinguished by their black hats and black skull caps, are commonly bearded, and may be seen wandering in the streets while intently reading scripture.

Do the foregoing types, perhaps with a few variations, constitute the 'religious' in any population and imply that others are not 'religious'? This would certainly seem to be a widely held view. Were one to invite a definition of 'religion' from passers-by, it would most probably be along these lines: Religion is belief in God, saying prayers and going to church, mosque, synagogue or temple. The corollary, of course, is that those abstaining from such activity are non-religious.

Durkheim must accept some responsibility for religion and its cognates being understood in these terms. He defined it as:

a unified system of beliefs and practices relative to sacred things, that is to say, things set apart and forbidden – beliefs and practices which unite into one single moral community called a church all those who adhere to them.
(*Emile Durkheim.* The Elementary Forms of Religious Life', *p.44)*

I find that definition altogether too narrow – as I do most dictionary definitions also. In fact, finding a generally acceptable definition may be one of the most endlessly debated and intractable problems for social scientists! So, what exactly do we mean when we use the word in a technical way, and its cognates 'religious', 'religiousness' etc? I come at this from another direction, strongly influenced by Durkheim, and put my case as follows. To me 'religion' is all about

modes of believing, behaving and belonging invested with sacredness, that make of one's life a coherent and purposeful whole.

Fifty years ago my eldest was in cub scouts. Before setting out on a trip to beach, zoo or museum, the lady cub leader would produce a length of rope. An end would be given to one boy, while she circled the group. Each would take hold of the rope, which would then be tied. Thus her charges would not fly off in all directions, come to grief under a truck or get lost! The function of this encircling bond would be to make from a gaggle of small boys a coherent and purposeful whole. Our word 'religion' is thought to originate in a Latin term that means to bind together. In my judgement, whatever it is that works to make of one's life a coherent and purposeful whole is his/her 'religion'. Now, look again at my definition above ...

WHAT DO WE MEAN BY 'SACRED'?

If the term 'sacredness' is central to this definition, what is meant? Is this just another conundrum? Not at all. In my early days as a sociologist of religion, the light dawned when I encountered the American social scientist Robert Nisbet (1913-1996). In making the distinction between sacred norms or standards, and norms that could be called secular or profane or utilitarian, Nisbet said that the latter were justified by their efficacy, their utility, or their rationality.

'Sacred' norms, on the other hand, required *no* such appeal to their utility, efficacy or reasonableness. In other words, what is deemed by people to be 'sacred' just ***'is'!*** It does not have to be justified. It is not up for grabs, open to negotiation, needing proof. It is 'off limits', 'taboo', 'taken for granted', 'given'.

When we think about this, we would probably acknowledge that almost everyone holds to certain modes of believing, behaving, belonging that (for them) come into this category. They are 'sacred' for some of us, although not necessarily for all. To illustrate, when the highly regarded Australian football player and coach, and fitness advocate Tom Hafey died in 2014, a sports journalist noted that:

> *Hafey did not drink or smoke. All his life, until very recently, he rose at 5.20 every day for a run on the beach,*

a dip in the bay and several hundred push-ups ...He never lost faith in sport's affirming and redeeming power.
(*The Melbourne Age 13.5.14)*

These modes of behaving for Tom Hafey were 'sacred'. Another journo, commenting on the early morning ritual, wrote:

*Not that Hafey is wearing a tracksuit. That would be against his **religion**: the one that gets him up at 5.20 a.m. every day, even if he's spent half the night driving back from **preaching the gospel** [my emphasis] at a footy ground anywhere from Orbost to Ouyen.*
(*The Melbourne Herald-Sun* 21.7.11)

IS EVERYONE RELIGIOUS, THEN?

The foregoing seems to suggest that people can be 'religious' over just about anything. Is this a reasonable inference? In the Australian federal census some citizens write in response to the question about religion highly creative answers, like 'Jedi-ism' (Star Wars stuff) and Raëlian (UFO's).

Certainly it would seem that people can be religious about one or other type of sport, such as Australian Rules Football. If you think I'm exaggerating that, look on the Internet for 'my religion is football' or 'football is my religion'!

Others again can be religious about cars – putting their all into the preservation of antique machines and affiliating with other people of like interest, or lavishing unconditional love on their newest and most glamorous machine. The Royal Auto Club of Victoria says:

*about 60% of men say driving a beautiful car makes them feel **confident and empowered**, according to an experiment by Volvo to identify how the brain reacts to car design. Volunteers were attached to brainwave sensors and shown images that included beautiful men and women, crying babies and Volvo's new Concept Coupe.*

The sensors showed men experienced more emotion at images of beautiful car design than a crying child ... .
('ROYALAUTO', Car Advice, November 2013)

Ouch! Being 'religious' in this all-encompassing sense is, therefore, not at all synonymous with believing in God or going to church or saying prayers. Hence this line of argument may not be very helpful in the long run, but we need to appreciate it! For the purpose of this discussion, we should narrow the definition.

IS THERE A POPULAR CONSENSUS?

For the agenda of *Two Elephants*, the focus is more particular. It is on those modes of believing, behaving and belonging that are by popular consensus **seen** to be the essence of religion. The majority of humanity, when this word is used, think at once about certain cultic practices, about some communal expression of these, and about conduct that is somehow reflective of this – like more virtuous lives as a result! Also (and unfortunately), 'religious' people may be regarded by some in the larger society as more closed, more critical and more conceited; to be avoided if possible. With some people, 'religious' folks have a rather negative image.

To illustrate, about thirty years ago I was 'locum' in a country parish whose young minister had died in tragic circumstances. In the congregation there was an elderly gent who had been a farmer in that part of South Australia popularly called 'the ninety-mile desert'. He recounted the advice given him as a young farmhand by his first employer – a taciturn fellow with an obviously jaundiced view of religion. "Just one word, son," he said. "When they quote the Bible at you, be sure you brand your calves early!"

It may be this kind of thing that partly helps to account for the oft-heard disclaimer these days, "I'm not religious; I'm spiritual." Fairly obviously, those who say they are not 'religious' are giving that word a particular meaning; for them it refers to something they don't indulge in – and maybe don't fancy very much either. It is not that they are consciously and overtly hostile (some may be), but rather that they are at least fairly indifferent to something they perceive as having little or no relevance to them. In the census over 30 percent declared 'no religion'. Religion as they would have defined it was definitely not part of their life, and they didn't want it to be.

"I'M NOT RELIGIOUS; I'M SPIRITUAL"

We will be returning in due course to the second part of this self-description (about being 'spiritual'), but for the moment must recognise that *indifference* to organised religion in this commonly accepted understanding of the term is steadily increasing in Western societies. This is reflected by the dwindling interest in churches. As I say, this does not necessarily reflect animosity toward collective or organised religion; merely a complete lack of interest. Philip Hughes, former Director of the Christian Research Association, assures us that Australians are more indifferent than hostile to the churches.

In the 1960s I headed a pioneer church-sponsored sociological research body; it was under the aegis of four Protestant denominations in South Australia. Among other assignments the unit was charged with conducting an investigation into the exodus from churches of older youth and young adults. Yes, this *was* happening fifty years ago; it did not start yesterday!

We trained a team to conduct open-ended interviews with a number of 'escapees'. These were asked why they had 'left the church'. There were the usual predictable responses about hypocrisy and boredom and irrelevance and so on, but one response that was quite unexpected was this. "I haven't left the church; it's just that I haven't been for a few years." In other words, there had simply been a process of gradual *drift*, in which one found he/she wasn't missing much, and could see no compelling reason to return. Not interested, any more! And this was more than fifty years ago.

The situation with churches could be roughly compared with the position occupied by concert halls, art galleries and museums. Only a small proportion of the general populace patronise these institutions at all, let alone with any regularity, but that does not mean that all the rest of us are against them or would want to be rid of them; again, the vast majority are simply uninterested, indifferent. Asking, "Why don't you take your kids to the art gallery?" would probably be met by, "Never thought about it, mate." Those active in the visual and performing arts are painfully aware of the fact.

REVISITING OUR DEFINITION OF RELIGION

We must resume this defining of 'religion'. When formally clad for 'liturgical' duties, I used to wear around my middle a black (or white, if dressed in white) cord made of three strands. These were a unity – each 'dependent' on the others, so to speak. *Entwined around each other*. Now, this is also the case with my definition of religion as "modes of believing, behaving and belonging that are invested with sacredness ..." They are like the three strands of that cord that makes of our life a coherent and purposeful whole! It is unhelpful to give priority in either time or importance to any one 'strand' in isolation from the others. They are intertwined.

However, in terms of how we think and act, it is probably accurate to say that beliefs normally precede and prescribe behaviour. For example, if I *believe* in the clear superiority of male over female, white over brown, straight over gay, these 'beliefs' will very probably be reflected in my behaviour – unless I am very cagey indeed. I don't need to trumpet from the rooftops these beliefs of mine for you to guess at the way I think. If I *behave* as a chauvinist, a racist or a homophobe, you will be able to 'infer' from that behaviour what I *truly* believe. Whatever else I may claim to believe is just words, words, words – but not likely to be the truth.

Those who argue that behaviour is more important than belief are setting up a false dichotomy. Behaviour reflects belief, so getting belief (which includes attitudes and values) right is a condition of getting behaviour right. All religions give importance to matters of belief, knowing that what we *truly* believe affects how we behave.

But religions, of course, do not leave untouched matters of behaviour, especially when there is a marked inconsistency between what one 'claims' to believe and how he/she behaves. Devotees can expect to be disciplined by their peers if this is the case.

The third 'strand' in the embracing cord is *belonging*. A fully rounded religion is a communal affair. Even a hermit is in a relationship of sorts with other hermits, although it can look very odd to those of us who are more conventional. You may have heard about the chap who joined a monastic community; one of those silent orders. Members were allowed to say two words every seven years. When this fellow's first term of silence was over, he was called before the prior and invited to speak his two words. "Cold floors", he said. After the next seven years, he said, "Bad food." Another seven years on, and allowed his two words, he said, "I quit." "I'm not surprised," the prior said. "You've done nothing but whinge ever since you came here!"

THE GROWTH OF NON-RELIGION

As we have indicated above, it appears that more and more in Western societies have no wish to be identified with 'religion' as they perceive it. Australia's 2016 Census found just over 30 percent of the population (7 million) saying that they had no religion. This may be compared with less than one percent in 1966 and about 13 percent in 1991. But what do such figures mean? There is much dispute among sociologists and social commentators, a proportion of whom argue that 'no religion' need not mean anti-religion, atheist or lacking any kind of 'spirituality'. It may simply mean disinclination to identify with one or other form of organised religion.

So, what of church attendance figures? In 1966 Australia had a population of 11.5 million, and slightly less than a quarter of them (or 2.6 million) attended church more or less regularly. Currently the population is about 24.1 million, but less than 7 percent of these are churchgoers. In overall numbers, far fewer go to church, despite the population having more than doubled. And even these numbers are probably inflated by the immigration of non-Caucasian people.

What about the rest of the world? Is the picture very different? Setting aside our renowned cultural cringe in this country, and adulation of all things American, I have argued that historical and cultural similarities with the UK should point us more in that direction for enlightenment and insight.

Steve Bruce, Professor of Sociology at the University of Aberdeen, reminds us that in mid-19th century about half the British population was in church regularly. The figure has fallen to about 8 percent, a little better than in Australia. But as in Australia, British churches are experiencing overwhelming and permanent decline – their numbers being maintained *only* by growth in migrant or 'ethnic' churches (as is the case in Australia).

Figures on strength of religious belief in Britain were not collected 150 years ago, but in more recent time these also show a decline – similar to that in church attendance. One-third of the population identify as atheist or agnostic, presumably meaning that the godtalk they think is promulgated in organised religion makes little or no sense to them.

Steve Bruce is sceptical about any theory, such as that of Diana Butler Bass, that some new age of piety and prayerfulness may be dawning. Hence the confronting title of his 2017 work. In it he argues that the new spiritual interests, albeit embraced by modest numbers, have been de-natured. In

Britain Yoga is an exercise plan, Buddhism markets mindfulness, Transcendental Meditation is a meditation technique. He sees all of these as secular therapies.

('Secular Beats Spiritual. The Westernization of the Easternization of the West')

He rounds out the picture of 'non-religion' with data from European countries and the USA; in the latter, for instance, churchgoing has fallen to about 20 percent, from 50 percent in 1950. The biggest fall-off in the USA, not surprisingly, is in Generation Y. One recent study has found 70 percent of Protestants in this age group (both evangelical and 'mainline') who were in church regularly while at high school had quit the practice by the age of 23, if not sooner.

Much is often made of Latin America as having the largest Catholic population in the world. That is true; it does have the largest Catholic population (over 400 million), but attendance at mass in Latin American countries is daily getting more like today's France than like old Italy. Fertility rate is a good indicator of the church's diminishing control over people's lives. In the 1960s the average Brazilian woman had six children; today the fertility rate is 1.82 – under two!

Hence the relatively new field of sociological research – into 'non-religion' or 'religious indifference'. This term is now accepted in academic circles to describe a specific mode of non-religiosity that is an expression of extremely low concern for religion. It is distinguished from agnosticism and atheism, especially militant atheism of the type represented by figures like Richard Dawkins or the late Christopher Hitchens. For further information on this the reader may consult NSRN – the 'Nonreligion and Secularity Research Network'.

IS 'SPIRITUAL' A VALID SELF-DESCRIPTION?

Now, back to that teasing statement "I'm not religious; I'm spiritual." We have established that this means the speaker is uninterested in organised religion, but *what* does he/she mean by the second part of that statement? The term 'spirituality' does not appear in my Macquarie Dictionary. However, 'spiritual' has become increasingly popular as a self-description by those who reject traditional organised religion. One study in the US reports that as many as one-third describe themselves as "spiritual but not religious". The initials SBNR are in common use for this category. "I'm SBNR."

The term is most widely used in the USA, and among younger people; it has not just appeared out of the blue. In April 2010 *USA Today* announced that 72 percent of 'Generation Y' considered themselves more spiritual than religious. Generation Y, born in the 80s and 90s, are today (2018) between mid 20s and late 30s in age. Journalist Peter Moore reflected a widespread opinion and media typification when he wrote:

> *common put-downs include lazy, debt-ridden and programmed for instant gratification ... portrayed as demanding and unrealistic in career aspirations.*
>
> *(Geelong Advertiser, 21.1.16)*

Regardless of how accurate that may be, it would appear that many of these younger adults still believe that there is more in life than meets the eye; that there is some kind of order of transcendence – whether or not they use the formula 'G-O-D'. Some sociologists have defined spirituality as the search for this transcendent dimension within human experience; as 'touching the holy'.

Having said that, it must also be acknowledged that being 'spiritual' means many things to many people. At the most banal level, it may be just another way of saying "I've outgrown organised religion." That is to say, the term can be used unthinkingly much as one might say he is 'Church of England' because that was the brand of Sunday School he attended. At the opposite pole is the insatiable seeker after self-knowledge and after some sense of union with the sacred.

To illustrate, 'Phyllis' (not her real name) became interested as a university student in Christian mysticism – especially figures like Meister Eckhart, Julian of Norwich and Teresa of Avila. From these she turned variously to Zen, Yoga, Tai Chi and Vedanta, to Jewish Kabbalah, to New Age psychology, also to Theosophy and even to Scientology. Single and a professional, Phyllis was not short of cash, and could spend time in California at the Esalen Institute and the Institute of Noetic Sciences. At the bottom of her garden was a room full of books, videos and CDs, and the heady aroma of incense. She liked to shuffle around in kaftan and sandals.

Phyllis is not typical, but she does bear some of the marks of that person we could call a constant seeker – as distinct from the person who is really just saying he has quit on organised religion. And, of course, there is a whole range of degrees in between. Some who call themselves 'spiritual' are genuine devotees, some are dilletantish, some use the word unthinkingly. So far as practice goes, the terms spiritual and/or spirituality tend to be associated with the private, non-communal realm – and consequently are regarded by critics as denoting fairly subjective, self-absorbed activities.

That is as may be. I find it rather unfair. Professor David Tacey, formerly of La Trobe University (Melbourne), believes there is a growing interest in this country in spirituality; he uses the somewhat extravagant term 'spirituality revolution', which I find yet to be proven. For Tacey this is all about:

> *a sensitive, contemplative, transformative relationship with the sacred ...able to sustain levels of uncertainty in its quest because respect for mystery is paramount.*
> (Tacey, 'The Spirituality Revolution', p.209)

Diana Butler Bass, a contemporary observer of the American religious scene, picks up the oft-heard claim "I'm not religious; I'm spiritual" and rings the changes on this to argue that the beginnings of a Fourth 'Great Awakening' can be discerned in the USA!

(Diana Butler Bass, 'Christianity After Religion: The End of Church and the Birth of a New Spiritual Awakening')

Having worked and studied in New England (USA) during the 1960s, I was familiar with tales of the first 'great awakening' and its pioneer preacher Jonathan Edwards. This phenomenon swept through the American colonies in the 1730s and 40s, leaving a powerful tradition of revivalism that would have periodic upsurges. Bass's optimism about a new 'great awakening' is admirable, but thus far is short on supporting evidence, as is definitely the case in Britain and Australia when similar claims are made. However, this does not invalidate her claim; she expresses great confidence. Time will tell.

Steve Bruce finds in the UK that those 'seeking' are more likely to be females in middle age or older, in professional or at least more highly educated groups (like 'Phyllis') and not proliferating hugely. As in Australia, it is hard to gauge numbers, but research in Britain shows them to be very small. Moreover, as he asserts in *Secular Beats Spiritual*, Bruce finds that most of the popular practices have tended to be stripped of their original character.

As for another great awakening or 'spiritual revolution', certainly nothing in the claim to be 'SBNR' can be seen as evidence that the old religions as we have known them could be in for a new day. But then, perhaps there is a role for something far more radical and exciting than the old stuff warmed up. However, we are getting ahead of ourselves.

CHAPTER 2

THE EARLIEST IMPULSE TOWARD 'RELIGION'

This chapter is all about 'looking inward' – to see what we can see! As a social scientist I have been just as interested in why people *go* to church at all – as I am in why they do *not* go to church, or why they leave, for that matter. It may be a reasonable enough explanation to say they go because of religious conviction, or do not go because religious conviction is lacking; even that they go because of habit, or do not go because of habit. However, that kind of explanation is just a shade too simple.

So why *do* they go to church – or to mosque, synagogue or temple? If it does not sound equally simple, or even more so, I have been inclined to think they must get something out of it. They are 'benefiting' in some way – or at least *think* they are benefiting. I will be returning to this. Meanwhile, I have two stories that bear on this question: one more directly and explicitly, the other somewhat less so. Here is my first story.

In 1967, while studying at Boston University, I felt like I was having a 'Eureka!' moment. I discovered the work of a psychology professor at Brandeis, the Jewish university a few miles out of town, at Waltham, Massachusetts. This was Abraham Maslow (1908-1970). In 1943 Maslow had written the ground-breaking journal paper *A Theory of Human Motivation*. In 1954 he published *Motivation and Personality*, and in 1962 *Toward a Psychology of Being* – sensational at the time.

The offspring of Russian Jewish immigrants, Maslow had grown up in New York's Brooklyn district, still called by some old-timers 'Little Russia'. He was a quiet lad, bullied for being Jewish. His best friends were books. He became fascinated with trying to understand human nature, and is renowned for his 'hierarchy of needs' which he saw as motivating us.

You may have seen his pyramid-shaped diagram that shows these needs in levels or layers. At the base are *physiological* needs for air, water, food and so on – without which we are dead. On the next level are *safety and security* needs, which cause us to seek homes in stable neighbourhoods, jobs, nest-eggs and so on. Next level again is *love and belonging* needs. When these needs for good affiliation are not met, we are prone to loneliness and anxieties. Then come what Maslow called *esteem* needs. By this term he meant the respect of others, reputation, appreciation; also self-respect – feeling OK about ourselves. Maslow saw the meeting of all these needs as basic to a good life. He said that we can begin to 'actualize' ourselves (be the best that we can be) *only* when these needs are met.

Rather like Jesus of Nazareth (who also was Jewish), Maslow preferred to focus on people's good qualities and potentials, rather than seeing us as fatally flawed and problem-ridden. He declared that our inner nature was not inherently evil, but either neutral or positively good. He argued that human beings could be loving, noble and creative, capable of reaching out for the highest. When they were not like this, it was because these **needs** he had identified were not met.

That is Abraham Maslow simplified. Needless to say, he would not have subscribed to that pernicious Christian doctrine of original sin! What he said made eminently good sense to me – because it seemed to fit with all my experience. This leads me to some of that experience and my second story.

In the early 1970s, back in Australia from those years in the USA, I worked with a parish that developed a sturdy adult education program. At one point, participants committed themselves for six weeks to work on the topic of 'helping troubled people'. To introduce the theme, I invited the director of a counselling service that was sponsored by the parish. I expected him to begin with a brief address at the very least. However, instead of doing this he said, "I want you to look deeply into yourselves, and put your finger on those things that most threaten, stress, worry and hurt *you*. Try to be absolutely honest with yourself. No need to share anything at this stage. Take a few moments for quiet thinking."

After this period of our talking to our inner selves, he said, "Now, if you have been honest with yourselves, what you have identified is the same for virtually everyone. That is to say, whatever most threatens, stresses, worries and hurts *you* is what most threatens, stresses, worries and hurts everyone. It is these things that we will address." I was reminded of a statement by the Swiss psychiatrist and psychotherapist Carl Jung (1875-1967):

Knowing your own darkness is the best method for dealing with the darknesses of other people.
('Letters of C.G. Jung', *Vol.1*)

My recounting this as a starting point must surely demonstrate what a powerful learning moment it was – as was my meeting Maslow's hierarchy of needs. It was equally so for the forty or fifty in my congregation who wanted to hone their skills for 'helping troubled people'. It echoed for me one of the oldest axioms enunciated by the Greek philosophers – 'know thyself' (in Greek γνωθι σεαυτόν, *gnothi seauton*). Variously attributed to Heraclitus, Pythagoras, Socrates, Thales and others, these words were said to have been inscribed in the forecourt of the Temple of Apollo at Delphi, and they may even predate all those to whom they have been attributed. They may be compared with that reference in Luke 15:17 to the prodigal son's life turning around when he 'came to himself'.

I have begun with 'know thyself' because I now believe this is the point at which those of us in the 'Evolving Christianity' stream need to begin in searching for an answer to the question "Is *homo religiosus* becoming extinct?" Why I have invoked this Greek axiom will become clearer as my material unfolds.

WHAT FUTURE FOR RELIGIOUSNESS IN AUSTRALIA?

My own forecasting pivots on whether or not the resources of organised religion as we've known it will be able to 're-constitute' – after the manner of the Phoenix. This mythical bird built a funeral pyre every five hundred years, incinerated itself and then rose renewed from the ashes. In passing, it is worth noting that some church historians observe giant leaps approximately every five hundred years. We should perhaps also remember that the new Phoenix came out of the old Phoenix *voluntarily* undergoing fire; not waiting for old age, infirmity and senile decay to take over!

Any way, it seems that churches have a choice between letting these processes take over – or voluntarily undergoing the fire from which they emerge re-constituted. The available evidence suggests that they are ambivalent at best. After all, churches are *conserving* agencies, seeing themselves as guardians of humanity's noblest traditions and ideas; this makes them inherently 'conservative' and resistant to change.

I recall a sobering conversation over coffee in 1967 with Herbert Stotts, Professor of Sociology with Boston University School of Theology. I was lamenting the slowness of change in Australian churches. "Jahn," he drawled (he came from Denver, Colorado), "You need to remember the religious institution is only ever crisis-motivated to change. That is to say, change comes about only when the status quo is untenable." And he added, "Sometimes even then it is unable to change. Logic is seldom part of the equation."

My qualified forecast is that, in the form to which we have grown accustomed, organised religion has a very uncertain future in Western societies (especially Australia), with the possible exception being some conservative-evangelical and pentecostal/charismatic varieties. I do not like saying this, for two reasons; namely:

- I am *pastorally* obligated to nourishing the morale of the faithful; not to demolishing it.
- I am *professionally* obligated to refraining from predictions that could become 'self-fulfilling prophecies'.

However, I have been making forecasts about organised religion for over fifty years, and have been seriously wide of the mark on only one occasion. That was in the late 50s; buoyed with enthusiasm at levels of churchgoing (a function of the post-war 'baby boom'), the impact of the Billy Graham crusades and the growth of my own congregation, I predicted a new ascendancy for organised religion! I soon changed my mind, and thereafter accurately forecast such developments as:

- The crises around faith issues for both laity and clergy that could be expected in the 60s and 70s
- The diminishing numbers of weekly 'pew-sitters' in local parishes and congregations
- The exodus of religious professionals in all major traditions over the same period, driven by a range of factors
- The declining numbers of candidates wishing to be admitted to holy orders

- The reactive 'right hemisphere' piety of neo-pentecostalism that would be part-generated by secular thought
- The increase in CALD ('culturally and linguistically different') congregations, with a predominantly conservative orientation
- The end of the old bitter 'sectarianism', and Catholic-Protestant convergence
- The decline of the three amalgamating traditions (in the UCA) from 1977 on
- The fading of enthusiasm for ecumenism as churches became more anxious and inward-looking

Although we were noting growth in the number of CALD (culturally and linguistically different) congregations, I did not foresee then the *extent* to which they might proliferate, and constitute a significant 'conservative' bloc. To this we return in Chapter 7.

In this matter of prediction, the onus of proof these days lies with those who contest my forecasts as unduly 'gloomy' or just plain inaccurate. Of course, most members of most religions have preferred to believe that their brands are indestructible and everlasting. These may falter and flag and fall in times of 'secularism' or 'godlessness', but they will *not* die.

The explanation offered for this confidence is that their religion (of whatever variety) is grounded in some kind of divine provenance, and has ongoing sustenance from that source. It is not humanly invented, but brought into being by the divine – who can be trusted to guard and guide it to the end of time. We have all heard this kind of rhetoric from our leaders. "God is ever faithful. God will not let us down." In my own tradition (the Uniting Church) this has been the refrain even through a massive financial crisis following high level mismanagement, and the corresponding tsunami of anger among members. "God will not let us down."

But this is a *faith* statement. It is not something that is empirically verifiable or empirically falsifiable. Divine or supernatural protection *per se* is not susceptible to that kind of testing. 'Belief' in it is something else, and can be very strong. We can, of course, measure how many people believe in it, and we can measure how tenaciously they hold to it. Indeed, we can even measure to some extent how 'beneficial' that belief may be to them. However, we cannot subject to tests and measurements the actual object of belief: in this case the protection of God. It may be true or it may not. That it should be taken as true (or untrue) is a matter of *faith*. It belongs in that realm we call theology, or 'godtalk'.

Social science is *not* about matters of theology. It does not argue for the existence of a god or gods, or for their non-existence; much less whether a deity specially favours his/her own, rewarding their faithfulness. It leaves all that to theologians, who have the most ingenious ways of argument that can make their case seem *almost* watertight (but not quite). Social science concentrates on what can be observed and measured – which does limit its possible sources of explanation.

As indicated in my introduction, the line being pursued here is strictly sociological; not theological. Wearing my sociologist hat, I propose to look at why people are, or are not, engaged with organised religion in some form. I want to pursue the theory that the original reason, in earliest times and in much of the world, no longer exists – necessitating a different reason or motivation for engagement with organised religion.

THE ORIGIN OF RELIGIOUSNESS

As far back as we can put together some history of humanity, there looks to be evidence for something we can call 'religion'. Pictures, dances, artifacts, stories, rituals, special places – and perhaps a class of 'guardians', all invested with some kind of 'sacredness', seem to have existed in most societies. Churches, synagogues, mosques, temples and other 'holy' places, plus what takes place in them, can be considered as expressions of this phenomenon.

It may be that some primitive societies enjoyed a higher level of collective engagement with religious things than we do today. After all, it was part of everyday life. That is to say, everybody 'went to church' – or did whatever was the equivalent of that. And yet, perhaps even in primitive societies there were varying degrees of interest. Quite possibly some, even then, were *more* involved than others in refining the dances, making the artifacts, adorning the special places, and preserving the stories. However, this is guesswork. What we do know is that there have always been varying degrees of interest in church, synagogue, mosque and temple life. Some have been more devout or pious, others less so.

While on this, a little digression into word origins could be helpful. The words 'fanatic' and 'profane' both have roots in the Latin *fanum*, which means 'temple'. The fanatic is one who is in and of the *fanum*. Since 'pro' means before or outside, the profane person is outside the temple. People have probably always ranged along a continuum from 'fanatic' at one pole to 'profane' at the other. If we take 'fanatic' to mean churchgoing, and 'profane' for non-churchgoing, this is fairly obviously the case today.

What looks to be happening, most noticeably in Western societies, is that fanatics (temple people) are becoming fewer, and profanes (non temple people) are becoming more numerous. Note, however, that this does not necessarily mean the latter are less 'religious'; it means only that they are losing interest, or have lost interest, in temple (*fanum*) religion.

But insofar as we are talking church, synagogue, mosque and temple, why are some keenly engaged? There are several ways that question might be answered, and they are all partially helpful. However, for the sake of the argument at this point, let us assume that people engage in most (if not all) of their behaviours because these fulfil a need – or at least are believed to fulfil a need. Look again at Maslow.

In passing, 'belief' (however nonsensical it may appear to us) of itself can be very important. In a congregation I knew, there was an elderly gent who was into homeopathy and herbal medicine. For forty years he wore a length of *red* flannel under his singlet and insisted on its health-giving properties. The colour was crucial; grey flannel would not have done! I was unable to ascertain why this was so – much less how it had been *proven* so. However, he had no doubts about the health-giving properties of this *red* flannel cummerbund next to the skin – and who is to say that he was mistaken? He certainly enjoyed splendid health for an old man and lived to almost 90!

Returning again to Maslow, we are suggesting that participation in organised religious life can be explained in terms of *need-fulfilment*. The participants find that this satisfies a need or needs – or at least they *'believe'* it satisfies a need or needs. Conversely, when they feel no need of it or think they have no need of it, there is very little to hold them. In fact, when one inquires of long-term non-churchgoers what they have against organised religion, the answer commonly heard is "I've nothing against it. I can't see the point of it." This is another way of saying that one has no need of it – or feels no need.

SURVIVAL

So, what *is* the need that calls religion in its most primal expressions into existence? This is at base the same need that underlies *all* human behaviour: the need to survive. The most elemental need of any living organism is survival. From the tree roots that find their way to dampness, to the little kitten that somersaults to land on its feet, the need or 'drive' to survive is ubiquitous. This is built into every living organism.

It makes us very early aware of threats and dangers, protective of ourselves and ready to fight or flee the enemy. Religion comes into existence as an aid to survival, or because it is 'believed' to aid survival. Indeed, it may well have continued precisely because it seems to have been effective in this sense.

There are two main aspects to survival. One is 'proactive' and the other is 'reactive' – to use relatively modern terms. The proactive has to do with exerting control on one's environment: manipulating and changing it to make it more habitable. The reactive has to do with accommodating to one's environment: adapting and modifying oneself in response to something we find we cannot change. Both of these responses are, of course, what underlie the process we call 'evolution': the proactive exercise of control and the reactive adjusting and accommodating.

In light of this, it is not irrelevant to contemplate that well known prayer we owe to the renowned US theologian Reinhold Niebuhr (1892-1971). It has been found in a number of versions, but this is how Niebuhr put it:

*God, give us grace to **accept** with serenity the things that cannot be changed, courage to **change** the things that should be changed, and the **wisdom** to distinguish the one from the other (my emphasis)*

The content of that prayer is both the irreducible minimum of successful living and the irreducible minimum of good religion. That is because religion was once and at base, all about survival – as was everything else our ancestors did! So long as religion is seen as aiding or contributing to survival, it remains.

CHAPTER 3

WHEN RELIGION IS NO LONGER SEEN AS ESSENTIAL

Once organised religion is seen as no longer essential to survival (at least, in Western societies), we are less likely to feel the same need of it. That is, unless we can find some *other* reason(s) to value and retain it. That can happen, of course. Let me illustrate from other, well-known 'cultural remnants' how this has taken place.

- Time was when a man walked on the outside of a footpath because this placed him between his lady and the wheels of a passing carriage, thus protecting her against mud and slush. Why should men today (older ones certainly) still walk on the outside? This has become a symbol of *courtesy*.
- Again: time was when a man offered his right hand in greeting another – to show that he was not carrying a sword. Few routinely carry a sword these days, but they still offer the right hand. This has become a symbol of *goodwill*.
- And again: time was when that sword was regular equipment for a soldier, for both defence and attack.

Without it a soldier would have been vulnerable. Swords have passed out of such use. However, they have continued to be part of ceremonial dress as a *'wardrobe accessory'*, thus justifying their retention.

What we have been saying is that religion emerges as an aid to survival. As it ceases to be crucial for survival, we either dispense with it or find another purpose, or other purposes, for it. This takes us into the issue of why people should engage today with organised religion, and support it, when it is no longer essential to their survival.

Religion endures just so long as it confers benefits, or is seen to be conferring benefits.

'BENEFIT' THEORY

The theory I am proposing here can be seen as a variation on Maslow. It is that much, if not all, human behaviour is motivated by the desire for and expectation of 'benefit' – of one kind or another! Once we move outside those things that are done because they are essential to survival, the bulk of our behaviour is *still* motivated by the hope or expectation of benefit – albeit unstated. Otherwise we would focus our attention elsewhere. This explains why supporters of organised religion stay with it, and others do not. Motivation research related to marketing shows how the quest for benefit underlies much if not all human activity – certainly the purchase of goods and services. Think for a moment about the way this works.

Generally speaking, we don't buy 'Krakelkrunch' breakfast lumps *per se*. Because they are 'flavoursome, nourishing and low cost' (so says the commercial), we are *actually* buying a taste treat, good health and money in the bank. Again, we don't buy the new scientifically-designed, fully imported 'Shuteye Serenity' innerspring *per se*. Guess what! We buy good sleep, cure for backache and perhaps even a better sex life. We buy *benefits*, in other words.

Pursuing the same line of argument, the believer who invests in Jesus may really be 'buying' alleviation of guilt, sense of self-worth and assurance of heaven. But since not all are worried about such things, it follows that not all will want to invest in the Jesus of some Christianity. Likewise, since not all have unsatisfied requirements for better sleep, better back or better sex, it follows that not all will buy the 'Shuteye Serenity' innerspring mattress! And if you are porridge addicts like my wife, no way will you buy 'Krakelkrunch'!

None of this is intended to sound either comical or cynical; much less disrespectful of other folks' faith. We are not into that. It is an attempt at being realistic and candid about our reasons for doing what we do. We act in ways that immediately, or at least in due course, yield *benefit* of some sort. If we do not think something will be beneficial to us, or if we try it and find it is not beneficial, we are likely to move on. Following this line of reasoning, we can argue that a shrinking number of patrons for a church or religious group most probably indicates that fewer people are registering any 'benefit' from their investment in it. Is that not obvious?

Like it or not, we are part of a culture in which an ever diminishing number of things seem to have what you might call 'intrinsic' worth, or worth *in themselves*. This can apply even to abstract ideas like ethical axioms, which we are told no longer have any absoluteness or 'transcendence'. They are just more human artifacts, and as such are time and culture bound. The worth of anything derives not from what it is or even who commended it to us, but from what it *does* or can do (for us). Medicines, modems and motor cars are valued for what they can give us; how well and how reliably they deliver whatever they are supposed to deliver.

Indeed, if you return to Chapter 1 you will be reminded that some men may buy a particular car because driving it affords them a sense of confidence and empowerment! There is nothing wrong with this way of our looking at things.

However, we need to recognise how it comes to be applied in the end to virtually everything, *including* religion. We also belong to a 'how to' society. We are absorbed with finding out new things to do, and how to do them. Hence, the new equipment or prescription or knowledge is almost invariably linked with a 'how to' outcome.

This affects the mentality we bring to religion. In a 'how to' culture that values everything by what it can deliver, inevitably religion and religious thinking are similarly assessed. We turn to this in Chapter 6, "Evolving Organism, Proximate View" as one of the major factors militating against support for organised religion.

POSSIBLE BENEFITS OF ORGANISED RELIGION TODAY

For organised religion to be 'marketable', especially today, its efficacy in delivering benefits to a consumer must be demonstrable and genuine. If it promises nothing, it will attract nobody. If it promises little, it will attract few. If it promises much and delivers little, it may attract but it will probably fail to hold. If it promises much and delivers much (in terms of benefits to the devotee), it will probably both attract and hold. This surely merits consideration, as just sheer commonsense – churches' great forgotten virtue!

If you are like some of my colleagues past and present, you will be starting to question this line as 'superficial', even opportunist. But consider this conversation I had many years ago with a colleague when he and I were both teaching in our theological school. I was airing concern about a particular student, who was rather boorish and bombastic. This could make him a somewhat overwhelming` package. My colleague said, "John, there are three qualifications for ministry. The first is commonsense; the second is commonsense; the third is commonsense. And that man lacks all three!" What follows is essentially commonsense, so please stick with it.

So, what kinds of benefit can organised religion promise – *and* deliver? Remember, if much is promised and little delivered, one cannot blame the customer/consumer for looking elsewhere. Following are twelve commonly sought intangible benefits from affiliation with any group or organisation – and in our case, a church. Not all will be sought by everyone who joins up. They are not listed in any particular order of importance. Futhermore, they would probably be differently graded by different people. Some will make sense to you, some may not. But all are significant 'benefits' from belonging – whatever the group or organisation.

1. **Cognitive Novelty**; i.e., new, fascinating, stimulating insights into the way things are. Sir David Attenborough's wild life television programs seem to have this down to a fine art. By contrast, traditional organised religion seems to be very accomplished at recycling the same old things in the same tired old ways, year after year after year. For those who like it that way, fine! For those who like *cognitive novelty*, it may not attract. Boring, boring, boring!

2. **Social Conviviality**; i.e. good connections with others who are not too wildly different from oneself; with whom one finds a certain mutuality, reciprocity and inter-dependence; with whom it is enjoyable doing things together – and on whom one can rely when he/she needs someone! In one of my parishes a man said to me, "I don't believe most of that stuff you say, but what a terrific bunch of people they are here!"

3. **Joie de Vivre.** That sounds better than 'hedonism', but it does mean 'having a good time'! It denotes the antithesis of a condition that medicine and psychiatry call 'anhedonia'; that is the total inability to register pleasure. Some religion of the so-called 'wowser' (a term meaning 'kill-joy') variety can be held accountable for promoting the idea that life was *not* meant to be enjoyed – much less, religion!

4. **Encompassing Worldview**; i.e. a way of looking at life that gives it some appearance of purpose and coherence – rather than being aimless, futile and messy. Not all are too perturbed about this, of course. However, it is one of the benefits many seek. Perhaps a slightly different way of putting it would be 'a way of approaching life with *faith, hope and clarity*'. Does being part of Saint Exuberance on the Corner help provide you with this? (By the way, she did exist; a virgin saint, she died about 380CE)

5. **Proficiency in Relating**. A study by Bell Laboratories found that the most valued and productive electrical engineers in the plant, working in teams of up to 150, were not those with the highest IQs, the highest paper credentials or the best scores in achievement tests. They were those whose *congeniality* put them at the heart of informal networks that would spring up in times of crisis or innovation. Getting along well with others is a paramount personal quality.

6. **Emotional self-management.** There is a wealth of evidence for the widespread inept handling of emotions, and their tendency to burst from cocoons where we had hoped they would remain docile. The renowned neuroscientist Manfred Clynes (b.1925) has identified and studied seven major emotions or 'sentic states' that he finds genetically fixed in us; not culturally induced or contingent. These are anger, hate, grief, love, sex, joy and reverence. Manage all these, if you can!
(Clynes. 'Sentics. The Touch of the Emotions'.)

7. **Inklings of 'transcendence'**. It may be that one key function that can still be well served by the institutions of organised religion is just this – and perhaps via music rather than in a torrent of words. My wife Lorraine and I are almost invariably 'transported' by music. Although the subject is outside the scope of *Two*

Elephants, it certainly merits our attention. Férdia J. Stone-Davis has edited a weighty collection of essays that bring together the disciplines of music, theology and philosophy. In the words of one contributor, music can be a significant aid in our 'effing the ineffable'.

('Music and Transcendence', pp.80-81)

8. **Self-enhancing activity.** Personal sense of worth is closely related to the activities in which one engages. Doing something eminently worthwhile creates and nourishes one's sense of worth as a person. Finding the opportunity to do good deeds that are congruent with one's capacities and interests is a powerful source of self-enhancement. Challenged recently to become a nursing home visitor, Millicent (not her real name) said to me after a few weeks at it, "This is the best reason for living that I know!"

9. **Physical wellbeing.** Aware that life may well be enhanced and prolonged if we are sensible, more and more people are seeking to know how they can monitor, care for and improve their overall wellbeing through alternative or wholistic medicine. Symptomatic of this is that allegedly health-giving supplements are a growing industry: of dubious worth to anyone but their manufacturers and distributors! *En passant*, be it noted that more than one-third of the USA's accredited medical schools offer courses on spirituality in clinical care. All want to be well!

10. **Effective Inner 'Gyroscope'.** The gyroscope has been used chiefly to *stabilize* and guide the course of ships, aircraft and missiles. In this context what is meant is the psychological mechanism that enables one to preserve a placid interior, undisturbed by outside buffeting. One well documented aid to this can be a form of centering meditation. The Zen Buddhist nun Kathleen McDonald says:

> Meditation is not something foreign or unsuitable for the Western mind. There are different methods practised in different cultures, but they all share the common principle of the mind simply becoming familiar with various aspects of itself. And the mind in every person, Eastern or Western, has the same basic elements and experiences, the same basic problem – and the same potential.
>
> ('How to Meditate: a Practical Guide', p.18)

11. **Positive Responses to Loss and Grief.** It is perhaps ironic that some of the funeral companies have been adding to their staff 'grief counsellors', and in some cases are also offering programs in dealing with loss and grief. Likewise, schools have taken up these issues, and also para school bodies such as Outreach Grief Services – offering help for children from four upwards, whose needs in this area have been long neglected.

12. **Effective Management of Stress.** Good stress (eustress) and bad stress (dystress) are encountered by all people. How do we distinguish them and control both? Staff of the world-renowned Mayo Clinic say:

> Some stress relief tools are very tangible: exercising more, eating healthy foods and talking with friends. A less tangible – but no less useful – way to find stress relief is through spirituality.
>
> (Mayo Clinic Free E-newsletter April 2016)

The list goes on. It includes overcoming trauma, bettering good relationships, healing sick relationships, discontinuing mistakes one has made repeatedly, getting along better with children, releasing the suppressed artist within oneself, discovering oneself through pen and journal, and so on *ad infinitum*.

There is, of course, a problem with trying to compile a list like this. Who can accurately, truthfully and clearly say what they want out of life – what makes life satisfying for them? Any attempt to codify or to 'bottle the essence' of *living life to the full* is limited by language. However, most know what they would prefer day by day to derive from life – and what they would prefer to avoid or evade.

The argument we have been presenting is that, only as the guardians and gatekeepers in organised religion are prepared to be attentive to intangible 'benefits' sought, and inventive in the way they diversify their product line, can anyone be expected to want what they have on offer. This is plain commonsense, and for that reason could be dismissed as simplistic by those who deal in more exalted logic – like the theological rationale for this and that. In an exchange via e-mail with friends and colleagues, regarding the so-called 'Atheist Church', the controversial psychotherapist and preacher Francis Macnab, then with St Michael's Uniting Church in Melbourne, said:

> *Much more crucial is the need to develop a serious study of practical theology. This is something the Australian churches have so long regarded as so lightweight that no one need think about it. But if religion and theology evade the practical translation of all the words into a Faith that works, then we might as well accept the attribute of 'a clanging cymbal'. The New Faith that I advocate has its basis not only in the words of Jesus but in the actions of Jesus; not only in the theory of theology, but in its practical implementation at so many levels throughout society. This sweeps into its path the healing of damaged personalities to the dynamics of conflict and violence, from the street level to a different global consciousness. As we demonstrate that the churches are once again relevant to the practical stresses and strivings of people and societies, the atheist church may be encouraged to be part of a New Faith that affects people in practical and relevant ways.*
> (Personal Correspondence to Clergy Network)

I have observed hundreds of churches at close quarters and conducted formal research in many to identify what makes them go well or not well. Those that are going well will be found to score high marks on at least half of the twelve benefits listed above. If they are not scoring well on these, they are unlikely to be buoyant. Call it 'commonsense'. What is wrong with that?

CAN ORGANISED RELIGION BE 'RE-CONSTITUTED'?

Some years ago I delivered an ABC broadcast talk called "On the Marketing of Religion". Subsequently this was rebroadcast several times. In it I worked with the notion of 'benefit seeking' as motivator, and proposed that churches needed to be more attentive to this. I said:

> *Let us suppose for a moment that you are not in the religion business, but fifth generation in a family blacksmith or saddlery shop. You can persist in offering horse shoes and iron clad wheels, saddles, harnesses and bridles in a world where horses are no longer the main means of transport or traction – and you can lament the wickedness of a horseless world as your business withers away. On the other hand, you can turn your inherited truths about iron and leather to the fashioning of wrought iron ware (doorknockers, fire irons and so on) and quality hand-crafted leather goods. That is what I would call an intelligent response to the market.*

Following this line, Christian dogma ceases to be something that is intrinsically good and eminently worth transmitting as a belief system, and becomes a primary resource for fashioning benefits such as we have sketched. However, in the form in which it has been received, Christian dogma needs radical reinterpretation if not reinvention! The distinguished Oxford scientist and Anglican priest Arthur Peacocke (1924-2006) wrote nearly twenty years ago that:

> *Even those intellectually-educated, thinking people still*

> *attached in some way to the Christian churches are increasingly hanging on by their fingertips, forced to bracket off whole sections of their religion as unintelligible or unbelievable in its classic form. There is an increasingly alarming dissonance between the language of devotion, doctrine and liturgy and the way people really perceive themselves in the modern world – a world they now see in the light of the sciences, especially the 'epic of evolution'.*
>
> ('Science & Spirit', July-Aug 1999, p.30)

Organised religion depends for support on its plausibility or apparent plausibility. How some things can ever be considered plausible is beyond me – but they are, just so long as thinking is discouraged or prohibited; just so long as patrons leave their brains at the door! On the other hand, if claims to plausibility are coming to be eroded, the whole edifice may be at risk. Part of my explanation for the decline of organised religion is that much of it is now seen by thinking people as implausible, nonsensical and irrelevant.

I had a discussion recently with the wife of a well known health professional. Both she and her husband are practising Catholics who long for some renewal of church and faith. I put before her the notion that much of good religion could perhaps be considered 'common sense' invested with transcendence. For instance, the Ten Commandments could all be adduced from common sense. They certainly do not have to be the private possession or peculiar realm of religion, much less of one particular religion. However, invoking the divine name gives them an extra 'cachet' so to speak. I went on to say that if anything about one's religion fairly obviously ran counter to common sense, then perhaps it was dispensable. My friend said, "That is what so many people in our church have been saying, although not quite in those words."

You and I have grown up more or less with the idea that certain items of belief and modes of conduct were authored in heaven, and were therefore absolute and non-negotiable.

A whole raft of challenges to that has come along. And so, now we turn to the issue of whether or not religious thought (theology) itself can modify in response to the foregoing.

TOWARD RE-INVENTING THEOLOGY

Theology – from θεός (*theos*, God) and λόγος (*logos,* word) – is the subject of divine things, or 'godtalk'. Its history is virtually as long as that of religion. That is because this realm of mystery, acknowledged in sacred story, ritual, place and so on, was *not* uninhabited! It was where divinity dwelt – in one or many entities. But note how even this attempt of mine at saying what the subject encompasses carries implicit doctrine; for example:

- That there is more in life than meets the eye
- That this is essentially 'mysterious' – beyond comprehension
- That an entity of some sort could be said to inhabit this realm of mystery
- That this entity – or G-O-D – is other than we, and we are other than he/she/it

In other words, the crudest attempt at saying what the topic of theology is about is already stating some rudimentary 'doctrine'. We cannot even begin to speak about the subject in a vacuum. We define what constitutes the field of theology out of some background history of religion, and quite probably some personal experience of it as well. That is to say, we define it 'our way'.

But a shocking discovery for some people, and still escaping many, is that *all* this talk of G-O-D is 'tainted' by who we are, whence we've come and the way our minds have been formed. 'Taint' has become a negative term of course (suggesting pollution of some kind), but it originates in the Latin word for dyeing – as in colouring cloth. All speaking of divine things is inevitably 'coloured'.

That someone (like me, for example) should be a white Anglo-Saxon male, born in 1931, educated to a post-tertiary level, married with six children and sixteen grandchildren ... and so on, constitute just a few 'independent variables' (as social scientists call them), which affect the way he sees, interprets and expresses things. Of course, by being aware of these characteristics and also highly disciplined, he can always to some extent step outside them, but never completely.

Therefore, the notion of godtalk (theology) being manufactured and distributed by superbly open-minded, inquiring people, value-free and with no preconceptions, is seen at once to be an illusion, a fantasy! This idea becomes even more absurd when a few other factors are noted. For instance, theologians acquire a huge body of *inherited* theory about divine things from previous generations of theologians. All this to some degree feeds into the way they proceed with the ongoing work of manufacturing more godtalk. They take over from the past, and build on this.

Furthermore, within this body of inherited theory there are said to be certain fundamental truths that are *incontrovertible*. They are non-negotiable. They become standards of measurement that are applied to everything else in the schools of godtalk. In other words, there comes to be quite a lot that is simply not open to criticism or correction. Rather, it provides the criteria by which everything else is now criticised and corrected. A prime example would be the Christian doctrine of the Trinity, which serves this purpose widely in theological circles, and within it what is called 'Christology'. If something fails to square with our 'Christology', it has no place. Let me illustrate with a story.

Some years ago, when my offspring were at school, I had some rusty downpipes replaced with PVC (polyvinyl chloride) tube. Several short lengths left over became useful playthings. For instance, they doubled as telescopes! Now, if you have ever held up to your eye a metre length of PVC tube, you will know that the image you see is set for you by the size of that opening at the other end. You can see nothing outside its circumference. Everything else is effectively, for the time being, ruled out of existence! It just isn't there to be seen. A prime example in Christian thought is Christological dogma; for the theological purists a 'prior view of Christology' (PVC) effectively defines what can and cannot be seen outside that circumference.

There is yet another element that sets limits on thinking new thoughts. It is that the majority of theologians are 'committed' members of the faith community whose particular brand of godtalk is their specialty. This means a commitment of the *heart* as well as the head. If they sing and pray on Sunday in a space expressly for worshipping the divinity whose nature and ways they are describing, then theology is more than an intellectual interest. It is their personal testimony! As my wife Lorraine Parkinson, a scripture scholar, reminds me, it can be much harder to engage in productive dialectic with theologians than it is with scripture scholars, who do not feel they are obligated in the same degree to defend a particular framework of doctrine/dogma.

One more point is worth noting; this is the professional jealousy and fierce protection of their work by many theologians. Believing that they are guardians of saving truth can make scholars peculiarly resistant to criticism and change. Stories abound of distinguished scholar/teachers who had little time for each other's work and were barely on speaking terms. You don't believe that? My dear friend and former colleague in Melbourne's theological education, the late Robert Anderson, recounts in his memoirs how:

> *two of the professorial staff, some time in the 1920s or 30s, had a falling out; over what I do not know. They were next-door neighbours with their residences in the Wyselaskie Building. One of the protagonists was Professor Rentoul, a feisty Irishman; the other was Professor*

> Macleish. They exchanged words only through the pages of one of Melbourne's morning papers, the Argus, which no longer exists. The figure of Larry Rentoul striding out at sunset to post his latest response to Macleish at the GPO was well known.
>
> However, it so happened that one day he was in danger of missing the post. Instead of risking that eventuality, he went next-door to Rentoul's and asked to be allowed to use their telephone; presumably his was out of order. After filing his copy by phone with the editorial staff of the Argus he returned home, a job well done. Is this evidence of eccentricity or is it merely a sign of bloody-minded stupidity?
>
> (Robert Anderson. 'Quite Some Time: A Memoir', pp123-4)

None of this is to say that theology and theologians are impermeably resistant to change; only that there are sundry factors that can militate against this. In his 1962 work *The Structure of Scientific Revolutions*, the American philosopher of science Thomas Kuhn (1922-1996) advanced the theory of 'paradigm shifts' in science, rather than steady development. A paradigm shift is a drastic, almost 'catastrophic' change from a way of thinking that has long endured – to a totally different way of thinking. A case in point would be when some of our ancestors discovered to their horror, with the help of Nicolaus Copernicus (1473-1508), that planet earth was *not* the centre of the universe! Thence came a 'paradigm shift'.

Commending on Kuhn's work, Paul D Murray noted how even in the scientific world resistance to change can be compounded by:

> *extra-rational factors such as formative training, personal investment of time and reputation, peer loyalty, professional patronage and the influence of ideological presuppositions, commitments and interests deriving from the broader socio-cultural milieu.*
>
> (Christopher Southgate et al, 'God ,Humanity and the Cosmos', p.73)

If this can be said of scientists, proud of their intellectual rigor, how much more true it could be of theologians! No surprise here. Writing of what he calls the 'unknowability' of God, Paul Murray observes that in spite of this being widely acknowledged, there can still be a pretentiousness about the theological world that borders on the endemic! He says:

> *whilst this (the unknowability of God) features as a traditional tenet of Christian belief, at the level of theological practice it is all too frequently smothered by a somewhat less humble tone rather more at home with certainties than it is with open questions.* (Ibid., p.87)

Nonetheless, forces for change are building. These are coming not in the theological seminaries and colleges but in the pews of churches around Western society. To this we will turn in Part II.

PART II

So, what is happening and why?

CHAPTER 4

THE FORBIDDING FUTURE

Although I was educated in church schools, like many a product of such institutions I was at best 'ambivalent' in my youth about God, church, religion and whatnot. Then at around nineteen I came into faith in quite a dramatic way, captivated by what had been called in the New Testament 'the Way' – before words like 'Christian' and 'Christianity' existed. My first ever 'devotional' book was *The Way*, by E Stanley Jones (Hodder & Stoughton, 1947)

Contrary to my paternal grandfather's gloomy forecast that the church was dying and I would be unemployed, I can say that I have *never* been out of a job, nor searching for one. In fact, I have turned down three times as many as I have accepted. I have enjoyed forty *paid* years in a highly invigorating and richly fulfilling career, and more than twenty satisfying *retirement* years that have allowed me to do as much or as little as I wanted. I have had parishes in Victoria, South Australia and the USA, and 'locums' in Australia and New Zealand. I have been a Christian educator, dean and teacher in theological schools, and university chaplain. I have been variously preacher, educator, consultant and writer – and, of course, traveller. With Sir James Barrie (1860-1937), I would say of it all:

> *Nothing is really work unless you would rather be doing something else.*
> (Rectorial Address at St Andrew's University 3.5.1922)

For professional development I took a master's at Boston University during the height of the civil rights campaign and the Vietnam War, and a doctorate in Australia. At Boston I was initiated into sociology, and duly was to specialise in the sociology of religion. Some research for the American Baptists in 1969 on what were considered 'slow developer' congregations in southern California fed my interest in church growth and decline, which would later become the focus of doctoral research and a lot of speaking – until hearers twigged that I had no magic panacea that would reverse the course of history.

But my grandfather was broadly correct. Organised religion as we have known it *is* sinking in the West as resolutely as the setting sun, and in the old familiar forms will be lost to view before too much longer. Can it be said that we saw this coming? Some did; some did not. I began predicting in the 1960s, and turned increasingly to identifying this now growing elephant in the room.

More than thirty years ago I was forecasting that the cumulative effect of *external* or contextual factors, together with *internal* or institutional factors, would be an irreversible decline of support for organised religion in Australia, the exceptions to this process being those we call evangelical or neo-pentecostal. Today I would add first generation CALD (culturally and linguistically different) churches, which are proliferating.

> (John Bodycomb. 'A Matter of Death and Life: The Future of Australia's Churches')

I suggested some strategic responses or interventions that might just 'retard' the process for a while, or ease us into a very different future, all of which were eminently feasible, but little notice was taken and little changed – reinforcing Herb Stotts' sobering comment to me in 1967 on what might change the ways churches operated!

At my predictions a few wrung their hands despairingly. Others dismissed me as a sensationalist and attention-getter, if not downright irresponsible – like I was putting a hex on churches. The majority took little or no notice, preferring business as usual. Today more are acknowledging the elephant in the room. The truth of the matter, which I am proposing to lay out here, is that the old so-called 'mainstream' churches in the forms that we have known – Anglican, Catholic and Protestant – will in Australia (and probably in most Western societies), be history inside the next 25-30 years! In the case of the Uniting Church, largely because of its demographic profile, this could be more like 15-20 years.

The composite 'Pentogelical' style (Pentecostals and Evangelicals) will be alive and well, although it will, of necessity, have matured in some ways. Indeed, this is quite evidently the case now. The big pentecostal churches are reducing emphasis on 'tongues, healings and feelings' and gradually becoming more oriented toward issues of social justice. After all, many of their adherents are getting older, and as has been the case with communities like the Hare Krishnas, this is reflected in style changes.

Putting aside for a moment the 'pentogelicals', among the general populace who continue to be actively connected, I suspect that a lot of churchgoing will be in essence for worship, or what I would call *turning on the sat nav and topping up the tank*. This is my metaphor for checking that one's life is correctly on course, and 're-fuelling' spiritually. I will return to this later.

I have not said, and nor for a moment do I expect, that religion *per se* will expire. Some species and sub-species of organised religion will certainly expire, but that is not to say religion will vanish from the cultural landscape. Indeed, it cannot! Churchy religion as we have known it will certainly expire – but 'religion' per se will not. Thinking people will be continuing to seek the 'benefits' noted in Chapter 3, and they will also be continuing to bump up against what we call the great 'existential' questions:

1. How do I deal with my own (and others') mortality? The inevitability of death. Is there anything beyond death? Does it matter, any way?
2. Is there anything to call 'transcendent' – beyond what meets the eye? Is 'G-O-D' a fantasy or in some sense a reality? Can we really say what this entity is like?
3. What is the best way to deal with the bad, the mad and the sad in life? Why do bad things happen to good people and good things (seemingly) happen to bad people?
4. How does one differentiate between right and wrong, good and evil, when making moral judgements? Are there rules, principles, guidelines that help here?
5. What does it mean to be a 'good' person? What is the best sort of person? How can I be the best that I can be? Is it worth trying to be good when many don't seem to give a hoot?
6. How can I achieve happiness and contentment – or is that an unreal expectation to have? What in this life makes for happiness? Is pleasure just a sop to selfishness?
7. What is the best quality of relationship, and where do I find this? What must I know about myself to achieve it?
8. Does any system of thought furnish answers to my questions – or are there really no good answers in the end? Do I have to suppress or ignore them, and just hope for the best?

These are the questions that won't go away – recalling for us that old chestnut about the Economics student. Exam time was looming and he decided to look over the papers from previous years, as a guide to what may be asked. To his surprise the papers rarely changed. He commented on this to his professor, who said, "The questions don't change from year to year, laddie – but we keep changing the answers." That's Economics for you.

Rather like Economics, these 'existential' questions as we call them, in their essentials don't really change. They come up over and over in one form or another depending on our age and stage of life. How we go about dealing with them is our 'religion'. Yes, our religion! Ditch that definition of 'religion' as believing in God, going to church and saying prayers. Religion is all about the way you and I try to fashion answers to these big conundrums we keep bumping up against – until the day we die. And although the questions don't change much in essence, the answers must and do. They have to.

But as it has come to be in my lifetime, fewer and fewer are asking these questions of *organised religion* – certainly as we have known it. When people do ask these questions, they put them to someone or something else. So, what does the future hold?

PREDICTION

Sometimes, when I speak of prediction, folks get twitchy, like I am talking about tarot cards, astrology, palm reading, crystal balls, tea leaves – spooky stuff. Not at all! This is all about the careful collecting and interpreting of data, and drawing inferences from this. Medicos and meteorologists do it all the time. To be sure, (where the weather is concerned) there is always this unmeasurable in chaos theory called 'the butterfly effect'. I'm sure you have heard that a butterfly flapping its wings over Beijing can affect the weather in Brisbane a week later – or something to that effect.

Among my big interests for 50-odd years has been social and cultural forecasting. The area that is probably familiar to most is social demography, which makes forecasts about population changes: birth rate, death rate, in-migration, out-migration, &c. This is critical for just about every type of human service: housing, roads, transport, schools, hospitals, shopping areas, city and town planning, power and water supplies, and so on.

Because I have what you might call a 'vested interest' in the matter, a major focus for me has been *the future for organised religion*. Since the mid 60s I have been making careful but at times unwelcome predictions about this. I confessed earlier to making that *one* big blunder before I had done any sociology. Buoyed by the success of Billy Graham's 1958 Crusade in Melbourne that drew over 700,000, by poll figures that indicated more people claiming to be regular worshippers, and by growth in my own congregation, I told a rally in the Melbourne Town Hall that we were on a roll; that God was sending a revival! In fact, this was the start of the great defection. Support for organised religion has been falling inexorably for fifty years now.

With that embarrassing exception, I've had it mostly right for over forty years. Mind you, I have often suffered the fate of Cassandra in Greek myth, who so infatuated Apollo that he gave her the ability to predict the future. When she did not return his favour and fervour, Apollo put a curse on Cassandra – so that nobody would *believe* what she said. Such has been my experience. Getting it right is not much comfort if people refuse to take notice; even less if you are dismissed as a stirrer or worse, a saboteur. I have been called both.

So, here I am, still making trouble by offering predictions. What I will say here arises from over 50 years of studying religion through sociological 'lenses', and from reflections especially over these last ten to fifteen years. To do this means our setting aside for a moment the fact that we have a vested interest, and assuming the stance of outside observers. I am not asking you to ditch your faith; after all, I have not ditched mine. However, I *am* asking you to think for a while like a social scientist, looking at this thing we call 'religion' in its organised forms) through different 'specs'. But there is another matter of definition we cannot gloss over.

EXPLANATORY FACTORS

If you retain nothing else, please try to keep this in the forefront of your mind. In sociology there are few if any simple, single cause explanations. If people propose simple, single cause explanations, their energy may be sadly misdirected, and their customers seriously misled!

Even worse has been the tendency to *ignore* some factors altogether (whatever they might be) and sell a glib and glossy package called 'Ten Keys to a Successful Church'. That is irresponsible and has led to no end of misery. It has left a lot of people feeling guilty because they have bought the books and gone to the seminars and done their level best to put all this stuff into practice ... for little or nought.

In 1986 I gave the J.D.Northey Lectures in Melbourne; these were published with the title 'A Matter of Death and Life'. I pointed out that the ups and downs of organised religion were commonly due to factors both 'internal' *and* 'external'. To take the former for a moment, we all know that an absolute klutz of a minister is very unlikely to pull a crowd. They may come out of curiosity, but they're unlikely to stay. There is a massive amount of data pointing to the minister or ministers being a massively significant factor in whether or not a church goes well. We cannot escape this. Neither is a congregation that is widely known as a battlefield of hostile factions very likely to attract; nobody wants to join a congregation where power-brokers are at each others' throats. These are what we call 'internal' factors; factors over which we might just possibly have some control.

But there are also a great many 'external' factors over which we have little or no control: things happening in the physical and social environment. I will be coming to them shortly. However, before that we need to see how religion, if it is to survive, must be an ever-changing phenomenon. Nineteen years ago Bishop John Shelby Spong published a book called 'Why Christianity Must Change Or Die', which not surprisingly drew some fairly aggressive reactions. You may not like everything in his book, but the overall thesis is correct. The choice facing every living thing since the dawn of time has been 'evolution or extinction'. It is the same with religion.

CHAPTER 5

EVOLVING ORGANISM – PANORAMIC VIEW

One concept of religion that you're likely to hear in some mission and justice rhetoric is the metaphor 'social catalyst'. A catalyst is a substance that brings about changes in its environment without forfeiting its own essential nature. Works in chemistry. Great idea. Love it! This is how some of us like to think about our religion. Always impermeable to the world's corrupting influences. Never changing. Indestructible.

Sometimes I have used this expression 'catalyst' when talking about the churches' social responsibility and role. But some find the notion just a bit 'twee'. After all, organised religion is only one of many players in the culture; let's not get too infatuated with ourselves. And it *does* change, albeit reluctantly.

I find a more truthful way to see religion is as **a kind of organism in symbiotic relationship with its environment;** that is, as some kind of living thing that has diversified over time into species and sub-species. These species and sub-species have emerged from the parent organism as responses to changes in environment; we call these 'adaptive' responses. Moreover, others have expired because they have responded 'maladaptively'. This concept of religion as an evolving organism is probably truer to the facts than that of catalyst, much as we may like that one better.

Author and journalist Anson Cameron, who writes some sardonic stuff for the Saturday Melbourne AGE, had a whimsical piece in 2013 on the evolution of divinities. Naturally, I would prefer to say that 'ideas' of God change, but this was his article. It began:

Gods die. Some by natural means and some by murder. Isis, born about 3000 years before Christ, was dead not long after him. Zeus, father of gods, who came into being when Isis was middle aged, didn't outlive her long. Quetzalcoatl was born about the time of Christ and reigned over Mesoamerica until the Spaniards killed him in the 16th century. In the North, Odin was born about 1000BC and expired in the 1200s.

("For god's sakes, our deities must get with the times", *AGE 30.3.13)*

Shades of Gotterdammerung, the last of Wagner's four operas in the 'Ring Cycle', depicting the destruction of the gods in a final battle with the forces of evil. History attests to the extinction not so much of gods as of many species and sub-species of religion. Long gone, for example, are ancient Assyrian, Babylonian, Egyptian, Greek and Sumerian religions; Maya religion, Mithraism and Roman religion, Germanic and Norse religion. All these were products of an historical period in human development. They emerged because they were needed, but when society changed, they didn't change – and hence they disappeared.

In 2015 the International Association for the History of Religions held in Germany a global conference on adaptation and change in religions. It focussed on the tension between innovation and tradition, the role of the individual as an agent of change in this process of religious evolution, and so on. This is a subject of great academic interest today – how religions 'evolve'.

In the past sixty years, the major sub-species of Christian religion in Australia have been undergoing massive change. Those that were left after the Reformation, that were flourishing in my own youth (Anglican, Catholic and mainline Protestant) are frail and failing – dependent for support on middle-aged and elderly, and with little or no prospect of attracting youthful recruits.

For most of Australia's history the churches depended for continuity on inducting the progeny of the faithful; not – I repeat *not* – winning hordes of outsiders! In Protestantism, Sunday schools and youth groups were thought to be the key, and in Catholicism the parochial schools. But that assured supply of recruits was shown at least forty years ago to be breaking down. Meanwhile, the sub-species of organised religion that *are* flourishing are those I sometimes call 'pentogelicals': once determined to maintain their differences (pentecostals and evangelicals), but getting to be more and more alike. Their principal source of recruits is from the disaffected ex-members of those old traditions.

Now, to some 'environmental' factors. Broadly speaking, there are two ways we can survey the environment religion inhabits. These may be called 'the panoramic view' and 'the proximate view'. The first is 'big picture', and the second looks more at factors closer to hand. Both are legitimate ways, although different ways, of viewing the environment.

First then, in this section ...

THE PANORAMIC VIEW

I want here to offer what might be called a 'big picture' perspective, which I owe partly to Karl Jaspers (1883-1969), unknown to me until I went to the US in 1967. Jaspers had enrolled first in law at the University of Heidelberg (Germany), duly switching to medicine and then to specialising in psychiatry. He held a teaching post at Heidelberg, where he was a close friend of the great sociologist Max Weber. But he was to lose that position during World War II because his wife was Jewish. After the war Jaspers spoke out in strong terms about the collective culpability of the German people in the Shoah or Holocaust. He said:

That which has happened is a warning. To forget it is guilt. It must be continually remembered. It was possible for this to happen, and it remains possible for it to happen again at any minute. Only in knowledge can it be prevented.
(BBC2 talk 26.8.2000, "The Nazis: A Warning from History")

At the age of forty Karl Jaspers turned his attention to philosophy and theology. He rejected traditional religious doctrine (including the idea of a personal god) but he was greatly influenced by some of the mystics, and also by Buddhism. He debated vigorously with the theologian Rudolf Bultmann (1884-1976), whose 'demythologising' approach to Christianity he disliked intensely. Jaspers' own freedom from any personal religious affiliation allowed him to look at religion from a very different viewpoint, which not all find congenial. He put his position in 'The Origin and Goal of History', published first in 1949 (in German) and then in English in 1953.

It was in this work that Jaspers advanced his concept of the 'axial' age (pivotal) for the period roughly 800-200 BCE – where he saw similar religious and philosophical movements emerging in Ancient Greece, the Middle East, India and China. He argued that during these six to seven centuries the spiritual foundations of humanity were being laid simultaneously and independently without any observable links between the regions where it was happening. This was an extraordinary claim, but it has real persuasive power with historians and sociologists.

Karen Armstrong points out that this was the time when

all the great world religions were coming into being. In her magisterial work *The Great Transformation* she points out that the systems emerging in the Axial Age all began with *a recoil from violence* (my emphasis), with looking into the heart to find the sources of violence in the human psyche. (Karen Armstrong. 'The Great Transformation. The Beginning of our Religious Traditions'.)

Armstrong opines that we are now in a second axial age. I have for some time believed something like this to be the case and that in fact, it is drawing to its conclusion. Following on her theory about systems emerging in the first Axial Age, Armstrong stresses that if a religion is to endure (at least *pro tem*), it should not only transform *us*; it should transform *the world* we live in. It should make a difference, and once it ceases to be effective in those terms, it will be displaced. I shall come back to this, but let me now – pursuing this 'panoramic' sweep – lay out what I see as seven main developments in what might be called the second Axial Age, in a lightning-fast survey of European history over six centuries.

- **The European Renaissance**. Starting in northern Italy in the 15th century and continuing through the 16th, this marked a galvanic recovery of human creativity; a 'freeing' of the human spirit unlike anything before it. It was a time when imaginative and inventive thinking spread over the cultural turf like a flood, and when the unchallenged status and power of organised religion began to diminish correspondingly. That is where I see it all starting! Today we take for granted the availability of print matter, forgetting that Gutenberg's invention of movable type in mid-15th century gave masses of people access to scriptures, together with 'emancipation' from the church's scholar clique. Meanwhile, sciences (anatomy and physics) and engineering made big advances. What we know today as 'Humanism' was born in the Renaissance. Nature was starting to become 'de-mystified', 'de-sacralized'. A process was well under way six centuries ago. It did not begin yesterday.

- **The Reformation.** Starting in the 16th century, this turned Western Christianity upside down, and stimulated a great range of religious innovation and diversification. It yielded new sub-species of religion that embodied (more or less) the so-called 'Protestant Principle'; that is, the refusal to accept any relative authority as absolute – as in an institution, a hierarchy or a book! Then, starting with the Council of Trent (1545-63), the Counter Reformation was the Catholic Church's attempt to put itself back together again after the sensational appearance of Protestantism. Some aspects of this can be seen with the benefit of hindsight as defensive if not downright regressive. Galileo (1564-1642), the Italian mathematician and physicist, was an unwelcome arrival on the scene at this time, with a view of the universe that put the church on the back foot. Indeed, the Protestant streams were themselves in some ways 'regressive', reinstituting their own set of 'absolutes'.

- **The Enlightenment**, in the 17th and 18th centuries, put the stress on reason and criticism over credulity and superstition. Leading figures were Spinoza, Locke, Newton – and, of course, Voltaire, who challenged religious absolutism with his memorable and oft-quoted rhetorical question:

    are we not all children of the same father and creatures of the same God? ('On Toleration')

    Darwin came later, of course: 19th century. He too was to present the church with major problems. The process we call 'the Enlightenment' promoted science, scepticism and hearty intellectual dialogue – opposing what it saw as nonsense, intolerance and a mix of abuses by church and state. By and large (and not surprisingly) organised religion was *again* forced on the defensive.

- **The Industrial Revolution**, in the second half of the 18th century, brought scientific and technological achievements that began to change the world. Mechanization and factories altered the nature of economics and of society, while urbanization and industrialization shaped both the physical landscape and the 'mental landscape'; that is, ways people thought. Meanwhile, the French Revolution, starting in late 18th century, affected every facet of French life, and much of European life. It has been called the start of the modern era, radically altering the way people regarded their rulers and governance, and giving impetus to freedom struggles everywhere – now well beyond the confines of Europe.

- **The 'Modern Era'**, from the start of the 20th century, has been marked not only by a vast mix of scientific and technological changes, but by the *increasing speed* at which these changes take place. Hence Alvin Toffler's unsettling work published in 1970 – titled *Future Shock*. Toffler made an observation then (48 years ago!) that would be even truer today:

    > *The illiterate of the 21st century will be those who cannot learn, unlearn, and relearn.*
    > (Unsourced paraphrase of a Toffler quote from Herbert Gerjuoy)

    Maybe that could be said to apply in religion! Change has always been with us, but the rate of change has been speeding up. The world of sixty years ago was changing much faster than the world of 600 years ago (when the Renaissance was starting and Copernicus announced that earth was spinning around the sun – not *vice versa*). This pace of change can be expected constantly to increase. Pundits tell us that before much longer biotechnology will have revolutionized medicine as we know it, and that nanotechnology and artificial intelligence will be creating a revolution in manufacturing.

- **The Colonial Period**, overlapping these other developments and running roughly from 16th to mid-20th centuries marks the export to and the imposition on subject peoples of the mindset developing in Europe. Paradoxically today, those expressions of European religion that are demonstrably withering in the West were during the colonial period being set to flourish. Now in the so-called 'developing world' they represent a major remnant of the old paradigm. The end point of colonialism is 'Globalization': the commerce not only of goods and services, but of ideas and habits of behaviour. The 'Arab Spring', starting in late 2010, was novel because much of its organization took place via social media *Facebook* and *Twitter*. That could not have happened ten years ago, much less twenty.

En passant, urbanization means that what the Canadian philosopher of communication Marshall McLuhan (1911-1980), back in the early 60s, called 'the global village' is today more accurately designated as 'the global metropolis'. That is to say, the world is turning inexorably into a giant city. In 1950, 29 percent of the world's population lived in cities; by 1998 this had grown to 47 percent. Demographers forecast that by 2030, 61 percent will be living in cities. Consequences of this include increased energy use and CO_2 output. In fast growing cities supplies of clean water, electricity, roads and sewage treatment often cannot keep pace.

In summary, then ...

Following Karl Jaspers, in taking a panoramic view over six hundred or so years – from the Renaissance through the Reformation, the Enlightenment, the Industrial Revolution, the French Revolution, the Colonial Period and the Modern Era – I am proposing that we can apply his concept of an 'axial age' to this time.

When we do this, what we observe is the steady and relentless *de-sacralizing or de-mystifying* of life, the *de-legitimizing* of authorities religious and secular, and the *dignifying and secularizing* of humanity, requiring a constant and continuing redefinition of the sacred.

Yet the fact of the matter is that apart from occasional 'bursts' that one can find highlighted in religious histories, this process of religious 're-definition' has failed to keep pace with the overall rate of change. Hence Karen Armstrong saying the old forms of faith no longer work.

Few in the world's great faiths (Buddhism, Hinduism, Islam, Judaism or Christianity) are managing very well the challenge of the 21st century. In the Christian world the unpleasant fact is that the old 'franchisees' (Anglican, Catholic and Protestant) have been caught with tired stock on their shelves that is mouldy, drab and unattractive.

God is still God, spirituality is still intrinsic to human nature, and people are still interested in questions of right and wrong – but God is looking for *new franchisees* who can package, market and distribute something for the 21st century. We are not talking about 'pentogelical' religion. This has been a useful response to the great mass escape, a 'stop-gap', but it is already showing indications of being a short-term and limited response to changes in the cultural environment.

With the euphoria over Pope Francis settling down, it is once again painfully apparent that the oldest Christian species (Catholic), with its headquarters in the Eternal City, looks to be crumbling fast. *Humanae Vitae* in 1969 sealed the end for its authority in the Western world, and if that were not enough, the hierarchy has been shown up as conniving, deceitful and unworthy of respect over child abuse, financial malfeasance and other scandals. There is much more yet to be revealed, but as a regulator of human conduct the institution has already lost the trust it may once have enjoyed, and the Pope's best efforts may be too little too late.

I beg my reader's indulgence for a sociological excursus here into this matter. The fact is that the Catholic 'general populace' in every society where Catholics are found are embedded in a tyrannical dominance of the *proletariat*, under an elite. In this system the concept of 'church' equates with the *elite*: those who hold power and who have perpetuated this by means of an impermeable set of structures and sanctions.

Social theory makes it plain that those who hold power seldom if ever relinquish this voluntarily. They must be divested of it by an uprising of the *proletariat*. Short of a revolution among the Catholic *proletariat*, the distribution of power and authority will not change.

It is remotely possible that some of the *elite* could shift sides to assist such an uprising, but this will be at cost to themselves. The only members of the 'gentry', or former gentry, likely to do this will be individuals like some we have known, including a recently excommunicated priest – declared a 'non-person' for his advocacy of women being ordained!

Meanwhile, the elite employ every possible means to avoid the abuse of children and other systemic misuses of power being exposed and dealt with. And meanwhile, the proletariat have continued to be too long supine and compliant, ensuring that the system will continue to be perverse.

From the perspective of social science, the Catholic system bears the marks of a tyranny. From the perspective of progressive Christian thought, it bears few of the marks of the original Jesus movement. This is not a value judgement on the many fine and (dare I say it) 'saintly' Catholics, but a sociological assessment of a system. Because this system seems impervious to change, Catholics have been deserting the churches in great numbers, and can be expected to continue doing so – short of a revolution.

We need also to examine the so-called 'Christian Right', including the school of thought that has been promoting 'Creationism'. As is the way with social movements, this looks to be fast creating its own opposite: aggressive non-religion. Insofar as the US could be seen as a 'bell wether' among Western societies, we should note that the number of Americans who no longer identify with any religion is one in five and growing: 13 million self-described atheists and agnostics, 33 million who say they have *no* religious affiliation. Drop-out Catholics are now the third largest 'denomination' in the US.

Adjusting poll figures for that well known phenomenon of 'religious perjury', Gallup says that less than 25 percent of Americans go to church 2-3 times or more per month; almost 75 percent are now not showing up much at all. In the UK about 15 percent claim to be in church at least once per month; fifty years ago that figure was 50 percent. The University of Aberdeen's Steve Bruce contends that the figures are actually much lower.

In Australia, towards one in every four declare *no religion* and less than 9 percent are regular worshippers. Using mathematical modelling, the American Physical Society recently forecast that organised religion has not long to go in Australia, Austria, Canada, the Czech Republic, Finland, Ireland, the Netherlands, New Zealand and Switzerland.

These are only figures, of course. It is the facts that we have to extract from any long-term overview of the changing human consciousness. What is quite plain, as Karen Armstrong points out, is that the old faiths are becoming obsolescent. I suggest later the nine features or criteria of a religion that may have some continuing value. The same tremors are being registered in Western societies by all major faiths.

For a monumental work of philosophy that approaches this subject from a different angle, one might consult Charles Taylor's 'A Secular Age', published 2007 by Harvard University Press. In it Taylor looks at the change in Western society from a state in which it is almost impossible *not* to believe in God, to one in which believing in God is simply one option of many.

CHAPTER 6
EVOLVING ORGANISM – PROXIMATE VIEW

In the last chapter we looked at the concept of religion as an organism in symbiotic relationship with its environing culture. I suggested there were two ways we could go about examining this environing culture. One I called 'the panoramic view'. In this connection we took Karl Jaspers' concept of an Axial Age spanning about 600 years, and suggested that we are now well into the second axial age (extending over 600 years or so) now nearing its conclusion.

But we said that another way of looking at the environing culture was to identify 'proximate' factors that impinge on organised religion; that is to say, much closer in space and time. I have five of these which are all fairly obvious, but are definitely not an exhaustive catalogue. They are not at odds with the previous theory; just constitute a different way of looking at things – which brings you out at much the same conclusion!

CONSUMERISM

Western capitalist economies are heavily dependent on ever-increasing consumption. No consumption, and the economy goes down. For consumption to be assured, there must be a constant mood of *dissatisfaction*. No dissatisfaction, and there will be no consumption! This mood is created and nurtured by advertising. Advertising promises *benefits* to the buyer. In a sense, as we suggested in Chapter 2, we are not buying articles; rather, we are buying *benefits* – like health and happiness.

This mentality of dissatisfaction carries over into other aspects of our life, including religion. Consumers of organised religion have become harder to please. Better believe it! Until 100 years ago the faithful were expected to go to church, to try to live virtuously, to put their money in the plate and to let clergy do their thinking for them about the faith. But toward mid-20th century a movement emerged mainly from the USA called 'christian education'. The message was that adults should be thinking and reading and talking and learning about their faith; being more sophisticated about it than their ancestors had been.

In 1961 I was appointed by my denomination in South Australia to develop what they wanted to call a 'DCE' or Department of Christian Education, with a mandate to promote adult learning. At first there was resistance. "We went to Sunday school and don't need more of that!" But by the mid-60s things were changing. Some of the structures we developed, like the church life conference and parish life conference, sent contingents back to home base determined to know more about what they believed and why. And they were getting harder to please.

This was when the bishop of Durham John A.T. Robinson (1919-1983) released 'Honest to God'. The Christian education movement looked like it could get out of hand. Adults were becoming more questioning and more sceptical than we could remember. We were sensing that the faith would survive only as it was carried by informed, articulate and intellectually respectable discourse. This changed consciousness has been part halted in the rise of 'pentogelical' churches, but will not be killed off.

The fact is that the greatest critics of claptrap in churches are the faithful themselves! For much of history a clergy caste has controlled the corpus of Christian knowledge. They are being challenged and questioned – not least by hundreds of lay men and women who have degrees and diplomas in scripture and theology. The *'consumers'* are harder to please! It would appear that the traditional God idea, for example, makes sense mainly (although not exclusively) to those who take flight from science and reason to maintain a fantasy.

COME-OUTISM

Intentional disaffiliation, as distinct from just gradually dropping out, has a good historical precedent. It dates from the Second Great Awakening of the 19th century in the U.S. 'Come-outers' were abolitionists who left their churches because these were seen to be slack on the slavery issue. The term gets its warrant from II Corinthians 6:17, "Wherefore come out from among them and be separate ..."

The 'Come-outer' movement was begun by William Lloyd Garrison (1805-1879), a well-known Boston figure who founded the New England Anti-Slavery Society in the early 1830s. Come-outers saw all institutions as flawed, churches included. They not only walked away from their churches; they also refused to pay their taxes, because they believed their government was corrupt.

One of their leading figures was the writer and mystic Henry David Thoreau (1817-1862), who said:

I cannot for an instant recognise that political organization

as my government which is the slave's government also.
(H.D.Thoreau. 'Essay on Resistance to Civil Government, 1849'*)*

In Western society there is a widespread and growing mistrust of institutions, including those of organized religion. Not since slavery, perhaps with the exception of *apartheid* and the discreditable record of the Dutch Reformed Church in South Africa, has organised religion in the West looked so morally compromised as today. Not to the exclusion of several other traditions, in which child abuse has been coming to light, I refer here to the oldest's lamentable history, which some now suspect could span a thousand years of ingeniously concealed clerical perversity. This has remained under cover because for centuries religious vocations have been shrouded in a mystique of myth and magic that has rendered them impermeable to criticism. The disguise has now gone.

To this massive scandal, which affects us all, one could add the Catholic Church's position on male ascendency and female subordination – albeit not the exclusive preserve of Rome. Scott Appleby, History Professor at Notre Dame in the U.S., has questioned whether the Catholic Church will *ever* recover from its loss of credibility over sexual issues. I doubt it.

The late Father Andrew Greeley (d.2013), the distinguished American Catholic and social scientist, told me over dinner that his church's authority structure began to fall down in tatters with the 1969 papal encyclical *Humanae Vitae*, which was all about the regulation of birth. He said (and remember this was 1969) "Forty percent of fertile Catholic women in this country are on the pill. They regard its prohibition as idiotic and indefensible." That was not all. "They infer from this idiotic pronouncement that its authors are idiotic; further, that if *they* are idiotic, everything else they say must be idiotic!" Follow the logic?

The Catholic Church is slowly and somewhat reluctantly starting to investigate why it is losing members in the Western world, but some of us think this is far too late. For example, a study of drop-out Catholics in Trenton, NJ (USA) identified seven main reasons. In order, these were the sex abuse crisis, the church's stance on homosexuality, dissatisfaction with the priest, uninspiring homilies (sermons), perception that the church hierarchy is too closely tied to conservative politics, the church's stance toward divorced and remarried Catholics, and the status of women.

It was this same report that said if ex Catholics in the US were counted as their own religious group, they would be the third largest denomination in the US – after Catholics and Baptists! It also noted that if it were not for the infusion of Catholic immigrants, especially from Latin America, the American Catholic Church would be shrinking faster than it is.

What becomes of 'come-outers'? Lifelong membership of institutions in general (not just religious) is giving way to *pro tem* engagement in clearly defined and achievable projects. Older generations provide most of the *long-term* 'joiners' in service and social groups. Young people, linking up by teletext and email, do not have to meet face-to-face to make things happen. When they do gather, this is for a specific end or project – not for the long term.

This socio-cultural tendency to *non-affiliation*, combined with higher mobility, is inimical to recruitment for organizations of most kinds, especially churches. 'Come-outism' is a new phenomenon in our time.

COMPETITION

The distinguished Australian historian Geoffrey Blainey says time was when churches exercised their role partly through their success as 'theatre'. He says that in the 1860s to 1880s, when oratory was highly valued, churches provided some of the best in the land. If one had asked a passer-by in Collins Street (Melbourne) to name the ten best speakers in Victoria, at least seven would have been clergy.

Today there is *no end of competition*. I put it to you that there is a vast range of 'functional alternatives' to organised religion, almost all of which have come into existence in the sixty-six years since I went into theological school! Allow me to cite four types of activity that historically were often associated back then with church life – and where potential 'customers' today have a wealth of alternatives.

- For those who are into **self-improvement**, and who 'Google' 'stress management', 'self-expression', 'personal development', 'inner peace' &c, the options are endless. You have counsellors, psychotherapists, life coaches, naturopaths, spiritual directors, plus a mass of inspirational/motivational speakers for seminars, symposia, conferences and other training programs.

- For those who need **support** of some type in tough times, and who are inclined to be 'joiners', there is a wealth of facilities like those I've already mentioned but also the more specialised agencies like Weight Watchers, Beyond Blue, Blackdog Institute, Grow, AA, Al-Anon, Recovery and so on.

- For those who have a **special interest** – such as art, drama, music, reading, spirituality or any number of creative pursuits – there is an abundance of facilities out there: CAE, Probus, U3A, neighbourhood learning centres, Yoga, meditation classes, Pilates and so on. Most of these have functions for their clients not unlike those which churches once had for any who were interested.

- Finally, for those who are inclined towards **service**, there is no end of opportunities. In addition to established organisations (like Apex, Junior Chamber International, Lions, Rotary, Legacy &c) and associations (like Red Cross, school canteens, Meals on Wheels and sundry auxiliaries) there are always vacancies for club leadership, sports coaches and so on. The endless assortment of ad hoc and established activist and protest movements present opportunities for self-fulfilling and self-enhancing activity. For the relief of human hardship we have Asylum Seeker Resource Centre, Plan Australia (Formerly Foster Parents Plan), Oxfam, World Vision, Amnesty International, Doctors without Borders, Volunteering Australia, all established in the last sixty years. For social action, Avaaz, Get-up, Environment Victoria, etc.

And we have not mentioned animal welfare activists like Animals Australia! The effect of *functional alternatives* to organised religion, competing as it were in the marketplace, has been immense and can be expected to grow. Now, how about this last one which has taken business away from churches? Wait for it.

In 1973 the Marriage Act was used to create the new category of 'civil celebrants', who could provide an alternative to religious celebrants for those wishing to marry. Up to that time 98 percent of weddings were celebrated by clergy; today well over two-thirds are done by more than 10 thousand civil celebrants. These also offer rites for baby naming, for the renewal of marriage vows, for same sex commitment, for anniversaries, blessing of new homes or offices and, of course, for funerals – plus ceremonies for scattering ashes.

Civil celebrants are *the new priesthood* – investing with meaning those significant moments and markers in human life that might once have found clergy playing a role.

None of these 'competitors' existed sixty-six years ago!

COSMOPOLITANISM

Some years back results from a piece of research on racial bigotry in Australia were suppressed and left unpublished because it was thought that the results could encourage rednecks, racists and ratbags of every stripe. The study identified four discernible groups or sets of attitudes.

- First, the *Conscious Bigots* – hostile to other races, religions and cultures; 'Alf Garnett' types, if you remember him. A smallish but vocal bunch.
- Second, the *Unconscious Bigots*. "I've nothing against wogs; just prefer they live somewhere else."
- Third, the *Muddy Middle*. Hadn't given the matter much thought. On most items ticked 'Unsure' or 'Don't know'
- Fourth, the *Cosmopolitans* – with openness to the other, tolerant of differences, saw themselves as having plenty to learn from the stranger. Predominantly young people, who had travelled.

The word 'cosmopolitan' is traced to the Greek thinker Diogenes. Asked one day where he came from, Diogenes said, "I am a citizen of the world." His word was *kosmopolites* (in Greek κοσμοπολιτες). Cosmopolitanism is antithetical to jingoism, patriotism, nationalism, exclusivism, any theory that says "We have the real McCoy. You need to be like us!"

Seventy-five years ago, in my school class there were *two* Jewish boys from long-established Melbourne families and two Jewish boys whose parents had fled Nazism; also there were *two* boys with Italian names whose fathers had come to Australia in the 1920s. There were *no* boys from other religious or racial origins. We sang 'Rule Britannia' and all but the Jewish boys presumed the world would eventually be Christian. We really were not the least bit interested in other ethnic or religious groups. I was almost 36 years old before I left the shores of Australia, unless you count Port Melbourne to Queenscliff aboard the paddle-boat 'Weeroona'.

First trip to the US, with my first wife and our four children, was by sea – on a grand old vessel that prior to World War II had been the 'SS America', plying the trans-Atlantic run. Not luxury – but much *cheaper* than going by air. For sea travel today, it is 2½ to 4 thousand dollars one way – on a freighter. I can get an air ticket Melbourne to Los Angeles for $1200 return; have a few days in Disneyland and Hollywood and be home inside the week. Is it any wonder we travel so much more. In any given year upwards of 7 million Australians will travel overseas. Distance is nothing; the planet is contracting. The official term is 'globalization'. Joseph Stiglitz, economist and Nobel Prize winner, defines globalization as:

> *the closer integration of the countries and peoples of the world ... brought about by the enormous reduction in costs of transportation and communication, and the breaking down of artificial barriers to the flow of goods, services, capital, knowledge, and people across borders.*
>
> (Joseph Stiglitz. 'Globalization and its Discontents')

All my twelve grandchildren have travelled overseas; that is still ahead for Lorraine's grandchildren, but doubtless will come to pass. Those at school or university have been in classes with a quarter or more non-Anglos – indeed 'non-Christian' if you pardon the term. Look at the prize list on speech night. With perhaps one exception, none of my grandchildren – nor most of their friends – are fiercely patriotic, nationalistic or exclusivist.

And what is more, despite being reared in the Christian tradition and educated in church schools, they give the Christian religion no superiority over any other faith. They are all fairly sanguine about it. They are a new breed; they are what we might call the 'cosmopolitans'.

CULTURAL CHASM

It is logical at this point to look at the biggest single worry of hardy pewsitters: *what has become of the youth?* It is little comfort to be told that in Western societies their absence is endemic. The Christian Research Association's *Pointers* journal has addressed this, setting down observations from a range of sources and figures from no less than 42 countries. What has happened?

The short answer is that there is now *a yawning chasm* between mainline churches and a youth culture that quite simply did not exist in *my* teens. Few of us back then pursued tertiary education; it was unaffordable. Many of us were in the work force by 15. We had to grow up more quickly, like those a decade older than we were – who had gone off to war. We married in our early to mid 20s. We had our families by late 20s or early 30s.

But in the mid-1950s all this began to change. Most social scientists date the start of a robust and distinctive youth culture to 1955 or thereabouts, when rock and roll burst on us. Youth knew the songs and danced to them. They began to develop distinctive apparel; almost 'in uniform' again! They had their own patois; ever changing to be sure – but it was theirs. They asserted a new sexual freedom. They were at odds with the dominant culture – not at war but certainly dancing to a different drum.

Today they're not hostile to organised religion; for the most part they're just indifferent. They see it as irrelevant to the lives they live. In many cases, as the offspring of an absent generation, who also see it as largely irrelevant, they have scant knowledge of the churches' faith and tradition, or interest in finding out. In East Germany there has been little tradition of religious faith for more than a generation; probably longer. Some Germans hoped that unification would lead to reinvigoration of churches in the East. Instead, West Germany has been getting more like East Germany.

We have noted that those who appear to have thrown a bridge over this chasm are the 'pentogelicals' – with services like pop concerts: pounding music, repetitive lyrics on the screen and super-confident pastors whipping them up like auctioneers. Teens are drawn to this for a while, but many take their leave – in some cases soured by the experience. Meanwhile, the standard Sunday gig in traditional churches reflects the culture that goes with opera, orchestral concerts,

ABC radio and TV, and wardrobes damned by the young as daggy. Young people who dig Wesleyan hymns or those of Isaac Watts are apt to be regarded as 'neanderthals'.

If you and I belonged to this generation, we would quite possibly not be in church. We may well be protesting on behalf of asylum seekers, demonstrating at anti-nuke rallies, and rattling cans on street corners, but not sitting humbly or singing heartily in church – unless it were St Isidore's modern mega-church! (St Isidore, 560-636, one time Archbishop of Seville, is patron saint of the Internet)

We inhabit a culture that is marked by change, change, change – which calls for continual adjusting. The fact is that the environment in which Australian Christians have been trying to do their Christian thing has changed almost beyond recognition. I entered theological school 66 years ago, and have been ordained 61 years. This makes me a 'participant-observer' over a period of unprecedented social and religious change. Allow me the luxury of concluding this chapter with a set of little snapshots to illustrate what my age group has seen.

- **Take the law.** Up to the mid-70s male-to-male sexual conduct was illegal; abortion likewise until late 60s and early 70s – in both cases varying by state. Capital punishment was still in. The last hanging was in Victoria, in 1967. Same sex marriage became legal in Australia in 2017.
- **Take the pub culture.** Early closing ended in Victoria in 1966. The 6 o'clock swill has given way to the 'pub club' offering meals and maybe entertainment; customers can be drawn as much by the gigs as by the grog – and, of course, women are not excluded.
- **Take the demise of wowser Sunday.** Sixty years ago there was almost no Sunday trading. Cities were so empty that the movie 'On the Beach', based on a post-

apocalyptic novel by Neville Shute, could be filmed in deserted Melbourne one such Sunday. Only Catholics played Sunday sport. There were few buses, trams and trains.

- **And take a sampling of new religious movements.** Ananda Marga, Eckankar, Falun Gong, Family International, ISKCON (Hare Krishnas), the Rajneesh movement, Scientology, Transcendental Meditation and the Unification Church (Moonies) have *all* appeared in the last 65 years.

Not surprising if people say, "Stop the world; I want to get off!" Back in 1970 the futurist Alvin Toffler called it 'Future Shock'. No wonder. But there is more – much more that is changing the environing culture, the rise of 'Chindia'. This is my composite for the two great Asian powers. In 2012, talking to the London School of Economics, Australia's Malcolm Turnbull said:

The rise of China and, following it, India, is a massive realignment of economic and, in due course, political and strategic power at an unprecedented speed and scale.
(Press statement, unsourced)

Anyone in manufacturing knows China can make anything we make, cheaper and better. China makes more cars than the US and Japan combined. The spectre of wilting industry, plants closing and jobs lost here and in the US for some borders on terrifying, and is reflected in voters' choice of President Trump. Between 2001 and 2010, 42,000 factories closed and 5½ million jobs disappeared in the US. Meanwhile, from 1980 to 2010 China's economy grew eighteenfold.

Turnbull has pointed out also that after 150 years of humiliating invasion, colonisation and exploitation by stronger nations, China sees what is happening today as *a return to the way things were always meant to be.* In other words, Chinese see themselves as justifiably moving towards ascendancy in Asia if not also the Pacific. In a disquieting recent release, the distinguished public intellectual Clive Hamilton issues a solemn warning: *"our naivety and our complacency are Beijing's strongest assets."* ('Silent Invasion', p.281)

Despite its horrific inequalities, India is not far behind. Aside from the economic consequences, there are inevitable attitude changes in a country like Australia, so economically tied especially to China. There could in time be a measurable degree of suspicion, hostility and fear toward 'Chindia' – as in those ancient days when the Israelites saw themselves under threat of foreign powers.

These observations are not meant to be exhaustive, but are merely recognition that massive socio-cultural changes are all around. What might be the consequences for organised religion are not easy to chart, but consequences there surely will be.

CHAPTER 7

RESPONSES MALADAPTIVE AND ADAPTIVE

In the last two chapters we have suggested that religions are rather like organisms in the environing cultural 'gloop', and that they can respond adaptively or maladaptively to change. An adaptive response equates with evolution; a maladaptive response with extinction. The factors dealt with in those chapters are now almost totally outside our control, but they are powerfully inimical to the long-term future of organised religion in the West.

Faced with this, I see three main types of response. One is the 'do nothing' response; in effect, just sit down and await death. There is an insidious version of this, which is to congratulate ourselves that we are the righteous remnant, faithful to the end! Whatever the version, this is the 'inactive' response.

There are also two 'reactive' responses, both of which can be classed as maladaptive; in other words, leading to extinction although not as quickly as the inactive response. Thirdly, there are what I would call the 'pro-active' responses. These are adaptive responses: major change that helps to bring about the emergence of a new species. So, we have a choice of 'inactive', 'reactive' and 'pro-active'. I do not wish to spend time on the first – because it hardly needs arguing that to do nothing is to hasten the end.

So, to two main types of maladaptive response. One is *'more of the same, only better'*. "Let's re-invent a church life that looks like the very best of the post-war years, and await the swelling crowd." Some who look back with nostalgia still believe this is a possibility. I see little evidence to support this.

The other maladaptive response is *'back to neo-orthodoxy and Nicea'*. "Let's re-claim Karl Barth, Emil Brunner and their devotees." In this case and with 'more of the same', the assumption is that what seemed to work well 50-60 years ago will work well today. Not so! Both of these responses are the last gasps of a fast expiring religious tradition. They are advocated with unquestionable sincerity, but are inappropriate.

There is also what may be classed as a third force; strictly speaking neither adaptive nor maladaptive, but nonetheless a significant 'non-change' bloc. This is the growing number of CALD (culturally and linguistically different) churches or congregations preserving cultures and bringing with them the theological formulations bequeathed by 19th and 20th century Asian and Pacific missionary movements. Few if any of these have access in their own languages to the literature of so-called 'Progressive Christianity', and there is firm resistance to any kind of thinking that might upset the old ways.

As these congregations continue to grow, their views – approving and disapproving – cannot be discounted. Until such time as a new generation, becoming more cosmopolitan through cultural immersion in Australia and its Westernised education, is in the ascendancy, CALD congregations are a gentle but powerful 'non-change' element, especially in Australia's Uniting Church.

I see **two main types of adaptive response** – very different but both sturdy specimens. One is what I have called the 'pentogelical' (pentecostal and evangelical) stream that is represented especially in the megachurches. The other is the so-called 'progressive' stream. My wife Lorraine Parkinson and I are not comfortable with that term; we prefer 'evolving' or 'emerging'; I will return to this.

In broad terms these two styles (pentogelical and progressive) tend to appeal to different 'markets', or different 'publics'. If I can give them names for the purpose of my case, these two types are predominantly 'the viscerals' and 'the cerebrals'. I use these terms *descriptively*; not implying that one is preferable or superior. Just different; that is all. So, what do I mean by them?

'Cerebral' first. My long-time friend Professor Gary Bouma, formerly of Melbourne's Monash University, and among this country's leading sociologists of religion, says that he finds so-called 'Progressive Christianity' to be overly verbal and cerebral. 'Cerebral' comes from the word for brain, of course. Used figuratively, it denotes things that appeal to the intellect rather than to intuition or instinct. It denotes what we sometimes call 'left hemisphere' thinking; that is, predominantly rational and analytical. Some people look to be more 'cerebral', shall we say.

'Visceral' comes from the word for gut, intestines, bowels. When we use 'visceral' figuratively we are thinking about 'gut reaction', emotion, feeling, non-rational, intuitive. In art, the word is used for work that has an immediate effect on the viewer. Contrast this with art that is esoteric and puzzling; that needs decoding, interpretation, contemplation. For 'visceral' you can read more 'right hemisphere'.

I am not saying the entire human race can be divided neatly into 'cerebrals' and 'viscerals'; not at all. That would be nonsensical. However, there is evidence that allows us to say that some are rather more visceral than cerebral, and some are rather more cerebral than visceral. As my wife or any of my family will tell you, I am a woeful mixture! I think I am as hard-nosed and ruthless intellectually as the most cerebral of my friends and colleagues – but I get leaky eyes at weddings, the opera and Welsh *gymanfa ganu* (sing fests)!

It is not our purpose here to analyse the pentogelical stream, or so-called megachurch movement, but I think that this is likely to have rather more appeal to the predominantly 'visceral' than to the predominantly 'cerebral'. It is not anti-intellectual, but neither does it encourage too much intellectual rigour. It has been apt to regard this as a bit of an indulgence pursued by overly cerebral people. At the same time, to be fair we should note a certain 'maturing'. For example, as we noted earlier, the importance given 'tongues, healings and feelings' in the pentecostal and charismatic centres has tended in recent time to be de-emphasised.

In contrast, the progressive stream looks to have more appeal to the cerebrals than it has for the viscerals, although the value of this emphasis may be exaggerated. I suspect that most of my hearers and readers are more with the cerebral wing than the visceral, and I want to address you as such, because this other adaptive response, of course, is what we call 'progressive', 'evolving' or 'emerging'.

WHAT IS 'PROGRESSIVE CHRISTIANITY'?

Contemporary 'progressive' Christianity (as it is rather unfortunately and smugly termed) is not at all a homogeneous movement. More correctly, it is a variegated stream of thinking that is slowly but inexorably spreading over the Western religious landscape like a river spreading over a flood plain. To call it a 'movement' is misleading – partly because its critics then ask for statistics. I prefer to use from here on 'Evolving Christianity'.

It is better understood as a grass-roots cry from members of all mainstream Anglo-Celtic denominations (together with those who have walked out) for a faith worth living and dying for. It cannot be quantified. Neither can it be denied or stopped. So, can we put some kind of a face on it? In general terms, it has three characteristics.

- First, Evolving Christianity says that there is *no* question 'off limits'. Nothing is so holy that you dare not question or challenge it.
- Second, Evolving Christianity says that there can be *no* literature, institution or professional caste above criticism. This is what theologian Paul Tillich called 'The Protestant Principle'.
- Third, Evolving Christianity says there is *no* formulation of the faith that can be considered definitive. That is to say, there is no 'standard' Christianity by which all that differ from it are judged.

Having typed the last three propositions, for some idiosyncratic reason my mind went back to the last time I was in the US. I was a member of a research colloquium in Cambridge, Massachusetts. One of the colleagues was a charming Franciscan priest. In somewhat light-hearted chat we asked him what he would do if he were to awake one morning and find he had been elected Pope! He replied that, wearing his papal mantle of infallibility, he would solemnly promulgate a papal edict repudiating the doctrine of papal infallibility – and would then watch as the Roman Curia imploded!

So much, then, for three general characteristics of Evolving Christianity – put as negatory propositions. To be more specific and more affirmative, what will come to be its predominant features as it continues to develop? Can we identify what its salient features are likely to be? This is where I may be going out on a limb; however, it would seem to me that the following would be the ten pillars of an 'Evolving' Christianity. I have tested them with a broad range of seekers who identify with Progressive/Evolving Christianity.

1. **It will affirm the reality of that Mystery which is for convenience called 'GOD', or by some Jews 'Hashem' (the name), without endeavouring to contain it in doctrine and dogma.** It will place a confident and intellectually respectable emphasis on the Transcendent – in whatever terms we elect to use, honouring the faithful testimony of other faiths and religious traditions.

2. **It will affirm the centrality of Jesus** as the God-informed person *par excellence* (from the late Professor Arthur Peacocke), as revealer of the Divine and as teacher of the art of living.

3. **It will evoke and energise humanity's native disposition toward pro-social behaviour.** It will affirm the essential goodness of persons and help them 'unlearn' what interferes with this. Recent research, e.g. in Yale's 'Baby Lab', suggests that infants as young as three months prefer pro-social and cooperative situations to aggressive and antagonistic. 'Original sin', as a doctrine, is soundly repudiated according to this way of thinking. Likewise, doctrines about salvation, atonement, redemption as classically stated have no place in Evolving Christianity.

4. **It will provide criteria for social critique, and energise the pursuit of just and compassionate society.** A major resource (not to the exclusion of other wisdom!) will be the ethical teachings of Jesus, as found in The Sermon on the Mount (Matthew Chap 5-7) and elucidated in modern works such as Lorraine Parkinson's 'The World According to Jesus'. You may like to consult also the US-based 'Beatitudes Society', which says its mission is: *to grow Progressive Christian communities for the sake of justice and the common good.*

5. **It will embrace the role of humanity as custodian and carer of the planet.** It will recognise that 'Gaia' (to use James Lovelock's term) is our only habitation, and the only habitation of our fellow humans and the animals. In this it will be informed by the classic directive in that mythic account of creation, where God commissions the man to 'name' the animals (Gen.2:19-20); in other words, to take responsibility for 'the farm'!

6. **It will hold before humanity, and seek to embody in followers, the dream of a functional planetary community** in which there is no place for hostile distinctions based on ethnic, religious, gender or other differences; the dream of a world at peace.

7. **It will be the warrant for a full appreciation of the body** – a valuing of sensual pleasure, the nexus between spirituality and health, and sexual diversity. It will not limit sexual orthodoxy and legitimacy to lifelong one-on-one male-female relationship nor treat other expressions of sexuality as deviant, or 'warped' – as some leading ecclesiastical figures have put it.

8. **It will strive to support fruitful integration of all intellectual disciplines.** In particular, it will take with absolute seriousness the ongoing dialogue between godtalk and science, and be unafraid of this delivering changes to its ways of thinking about God, humanity and the cosmos.

9. **It will promote and inform the 'journey inward'**, gathering and disseminating insights into touching transcendence, placing a high value on practices of introspection, contemplation, meditation, mindfulness.

10. **It will find ways, intellectually and aesthetically worthy, for collective celebration of the foregoing**, based on the conviction that:

*THE IRREDUCIBLE MINIMUM
FOR A RELIGIOUS COMMUNITY
IS THE RITUAL OF SUBLIMITY:
THE EVENT IN WHICH MEMBERS
REACH UP SYMBOLICALLY
TO THE HIGHEST THEY KNOW
AND WHICH ORIENTS THEM
TO THIS WHEN THEY DISPERSE*

Anything less than the propositions listed above cannot be called 'Evolving Christianity'. It may be sincerely and passionately held, but should probably be called something else!

A propos #10 ... I recall a chat some years ago with a well known layman, whom I had known since his teens. He and his wife had moved from the congregation in which they grew up to a much bigger one in the city. I knew there must be good reasons, and asked what these were. I should explain that he held a key post in a federal government agency; she was a medical practitioner. They had school age offspring. In answer to my question, he said:

"You know the demands our work puts on us. In addition, J.... is on the school board and I'm in the local branch of the party. We take the kids to music and sport. We're not able to teach in Sunday school, help with youth group, join choirs and committees or go to socials. **We want a place that puts us consciously in touch with Transcendence and helps us get our heads in order.** *(my emphasis) We like the worship there because it does that for us."*

Now, back to a point I made earlier. I said then that those who haven't bought into pentogelical churches, but who are still after something, will quite probably be those who are wanting to *switch on the sat nav and top up the tank*, to use a metaphor from travelling. Or, in other words, to check their life's direction against some order of transcendence, and to lay hold on the dynamic that will empower them for another week.

In fact, this is what my wife and I want from gathered life in church. We are enmeshed in a tangle of responsibilities in the world. Like many who will be reading this, we have money taken out of our bank account every month for major NGOs and we belong to sundry organizations that exist to make the world better. For us the irreducible minimum of gathered life is to *switch on the sat nav and top up the tank*.

I am not saying that this should be all church is or does, nor that it is all a person should want or draw from being 'church'. But I understand those who say *"What I want is a context for getting 'God-informed' in the way Jesus was, in the hope that I might be able to call myself a follower of the Way."*

On our travels, a high point for Lorraine and me has been a choral evensong in a cathedral. We have felt consciously in touch with Transcendence in a way that seldom happens in a standard Sunday filibuster. It would seem that many may be still searching for something like this.

PART III

The Future for Religious Leadership

CHAPTER 8

THE EMERGING RELIGIOUS PROFESSIONAL

In April 2010 a letter went to Uniting Church ministers in Victoria and Tasmania from the Synod General Secretary, advising that a 'task group' had been set up to address the decreasing number of candidates offering for ordained ministry. It intimated that 'various groups' (unspecified) at Synod and Assembly levels were undertaking further work.

Three years on, and having heard nothing, I made inquiries – and was pleased then to receive a report on the work done. It was entitled 'Creating a Culture of Call', but in my judgement failed dismally to recognise what these last seven chapters have been setting down. I seriously doubt that those given the assignment took much account of cataclysmic changes since I offered as a candidate for ordination and was accepted, in 1951. Back then there was broad consensus in churches, and to some extent also in society at large, about three things:

- What the ecclesiastical *and* 'cultural' roles of clergy were,
- What kind of personal and professional equipment would best ensure the discharge of these roles, and

- What sort of human beings were most likely to be fitted for these roles.

That consensus has gone. The larger society has little or no interest in what clergy should be and do; also, clergy no longer enjoy the regard and trust that existed then – and any remaining esteem is ebbing away fast. They are widely regarded as rather quaint old relics of bygone time, as is abundantly clear in the way they are typified (or caricatured) in film and TV.

In 2014 my former colleague in university chaplaincy Father Michael Elligate was named in the Australia Day honours, prompting a journalist to write, "When he walks around the university and the three hospitals near his church, Father Michael Elligate wears casual slacks and a shirt, rather than his priest's robes." Aside from the fact that Michael's apparel is irrelevant to his receiving a national honour, the journalist's stereotype cleric would seem to stand out in a crowd for his eccentricities and social awkwardness.

Churches themselves are unclear on the three considerations I have mentioned. We are not hearing anything enlightening on: What sort of people are we looking for? How do we think they can be best equipped? and What are we expecting them to do?

Twenty years ago I completed a study commissioned by the Victorian Synod of the Uniting Church into what laity looked for in ministers. Twelve presbyteries (regions) gathered 'focus groups' of lay people with whom I met. A report called 'On Whom Hands are Laid' was informative but has had little effect on recruitment and selection.

The facts are that few today could state clearly and concisely what ordained ministries or 'designated professional leaders' may be expected to do in the next ten years, much less twenty, and hence they fall back on old models, including the shape of theological education. I shall come to that in a moment.

So long as this lack of clarity exists, it is no wonder that men and women who at another time may have offered for the ordained ministry are looking elsewhere for ways to serve God and humanity. Also, it is no wonder if families and clergy, far from pointing such people to theological colleges/seminaries, are pointing them away. I have had many older colleagues say to me that they would *not* offer today for ordained ministry, and moreover that they would *not* encourage others to do so. What then for the religious professional of the future?

There are three parts in what I propose to say on this. I want to deal with the issue under these headings. The first is 'The Tyranny of Tradition', the second is 'Reminders of the Sublime' and the third is 'The Edison-Tillich Type'.

THE TYRANNY OF TRADITION

> *Theological training today is not radically different from that which was given fifty years ago. Knowledge of Biblical languages, of dogmatics, and Church history still form its main outline. Psychology and the study of religion are usually mere sidelines. The average theological student knows very little indeed of religion except in its Hebrew and Christian expressions. In days when it was thought that these alone represented God's revelation and the religions of other races were idolatrous superstition, this might be justified. It cannot be justified today.*
> (Waterhouse, 'The Dawn of Religion', p.10)

Who said that? It was written by Eric Waterhouse, Professor of the Philosophy of Religion at the University of London – in 1936! Some things never change.

Forty years on, in 1976, while working in an industrial satellite city in South Australia, I received an unexpected and unsought overture. I was sounded out to be 'dean-designate' of the Uniting Church's theological school in Melbourne, which would come into being with union in 1977 of the Congregational, Methodist and Presbyterian churches.

Following much agonising I let my name go forward, and was duly appointed – for life if I wished. After ten very satisfying years, but somewhat disillusioned, I moved on. Let me explain with this episode.

Soon after union all UCA institutions of theological education were asked by the national Assembly to conduct a curriculum review. I proposed to colleagues a type of Geoffrey Robertson 'hypothetical'. This was that we imagine ourselves in some hard-line repressive state with religious life restricted at every turn. In this environment we were allowed to run a seminary and to take candidates away from factory or farm for not more than 12 months. Then they had to resume 'gainful' work. They could do their religious thing in such free time as they had. Violation of these restrictions could find us all in the salt mines! I suggested that it might be an interesting exercise to imagine ourselves in this situation, and to ask two questions.

- First, what in the circumstances would we see as the irreducible minima of 'ministry' (as we have called it)?
- Second, given this, what would be the irreducible minima of personal and professional equipment for this?

It seemed to me that *only* by employing a 'forcing' device like this would we have some chance of breaking through to the essentials. Not surprisingly, the outrageous nature of the exercise brought it undone; most of my colleagues thought I was loopy. Not to proffer answers to my questions, but to rebut the whole exercise, a former colleague (now deceased) said:

"*We need to remember that we work within certain parameters ...*

- *One, a body of our Assembly ('Ministerial Education Council') sets down the requirements for ordination;*
- *Two, a body of our Synod ('Board of Ministerial Education') is our direct line of accountability to the church;*

- Three, we are a party in a tri-denomination consortium ('United Faculty of Theology');
- Four, we are committed to teaching for degrees granted by another ecumenical body ('Melbourne College of Divinity')
- Five, we have a body of academics with specialties and we have commissioned them to induct candidates for ministry into these disciplines ... (dramatic pause)"

He concluded by saying, "Within these parameters we are free to do anything we like!"

Boom! Of course, my hypothetical should have fallen flat, because it was suggesting a scenario where the entire structure of theological education (degrees and all) may have to be abandoned. No wonder that colleagues rejected it. To the best of my knowledge, my two questions remained unanswered, and I am not aware that they have ever been seriously addressed – at least in the way I put them. If my colleagues saw themselves preparing candidates for 'ministry', it appeared that this was always secondary to their teaching toward a degree in theology.

The late Sir John Templeton (1912-2008), American financier and philanthropist, and founder of the annual prize for progress in religion that bears his name, was a Presbyterian elder in the US and was 42 years on the board of trustees of Princeton Theological Seminary. Sir John commented sadly of those years with Princeton that:

> We had brilliant people – teachers and students both – but they did not come up with many new concepts. They weren't invited to come up with new concepts. Anybody who had come up with a new concept would have been under suspicion for being out of step with the tradition or out of step with the teachings of the church.
>
> (The Quotable Sir John – On Life and Spirituality)

In Australia, the last thirty years have seen church

membership shrink, congregations close, the number of active ministers drop, and likewise the number of candidates preparing for ordination. On the membership issue, when people point to the growth in 'pentogelical' religion, I remind them that three-quarters of that growth is due to the reclamation of refugees and drop-outs from other churches.

We may be confident in saying that the fall-off in candidates reflects, among other things, our uncertainty about what religious professionals might be doing in the next 10-15 years. There seems to be an assumption that we can look to the past for operational models and for the content of theological education, but this is only because we are unsure what else to say!

As Dean of our theological school from 1977-86, it fell to me to interview students at length during their final year. This included my inviting them to talk about the concept of ministry they had formed during the years of preparation. We would run through a mix of terms one might expect to hear – like evangelist, leader, pastor, administrator, educator, priest, counsellor, preacher, rabbi, 'enabler' (that was trendy for a while) and others. We would discuss which word might work as an umbrella term that covered all the others, or which word packaged the topmost priority. There was one term that I cannot recall *ever* being canvassed. So, what was this other term?

GUARDING REMINDERS OF THE SUBLIME

In 1988 I was approached to be full-time 'ecumenical chaplain' with the University of Melbourne. At the time I was exploring other options, and I hedged on this as I had done twelve years earlier with an invitation to the theological hall. I was duly appointed, and one of the first things I did was to look for the origin of the word 'chaplain'. I had heard it used of religious professionals in schools, hospitals, armed services, factories; of any job *not* parish-based (or "not the *real* ministry"). But how many know the origin of the word? Like many stories tinged with mystique, it has probably been subject to some editing, but so far as we can gather, these are the facts.

In the 4th century a young member of the Roman cavalry named Martin (c316-397), who had been taking instruction in the new religion of Empire, was stationed outside what is today's Amiens in France. One chilly night he was confronted by a near naked beggar. Martin cut his huge cavalry cloak in two and threw half around the beggar. That night in a dream he saw Jesus wearing the half of his cloak and heard him say, "The Roman soldier Martin has given this to me." He was duly baptised, and told his commander that as a Christian he could not take up arms. Shortly after this Martin was discharged from the cavalry.

He became a monk, renowned for his simple life and compassion with the needy. Eventually Martin became Bishop of Tours in France. When he died in the year 397, the remaining half of his *cappella* (or cloak) was kept as a holy relic, and the shrine where it was guarded took on the name of the cloak. The French took the word into their language as *chapèle*, which gives us *chapel*. The guardian of Martin's cloak was called *cappellanus*, which became *chapelain* in old French, and in English, *chaplain*!

Etymologically speaking, a chaplain is one who guards reminders of the 'sublime' amid the secular. That word deserves explanation. Sublime originates in the Latin *sublimis*, from *sub* meaning 'up to', and *limen* meaning 'lintel' (top of a doorway). Sublime came to mean raised up, held aloft, soaring, lofty, exalted. We think of it as denoting things of high moral, intellectual or spiritual degree, and things that inspire awe, wonder, reverence; 'sublime' sentiments (like a glimpse of Martin's cloak!)

As custodian or guardian of such things, obviously the *cappellanus* will be both a listener and a story-teller. When the pilgrims paused at Tours, this would be to share with the *cappellanus* accounts of their journeying, and to hear stories and teachings associated with the saintly Martin. They would take again to the road, now bearing with them what was mediated by the *cappellanus*. He had heard them, he had told them stories, and he had sent them on their way with a spring in the step and a song in the heart.

Now, a slight deviation. In 2003, under pressure from students I had taught and from the notable Australian preacher Gordon Powell, I completed 'Excited to Speak, Exciting to Hear', sub-titled 'the art of preaching'. One former student said, "Best book on preaching I have read; only one thing wrong with it." "What is that?" "Twenty years too late!" My hesitation to write had come precisely from the impression that clergy were no longer interested in fashioning a story that might put a spring in the step and a song in the heart; otherwise, 'excite' hearers because it 'excited' them.

In 'Excited to Speak, Exciting to Hear', I suggested that too many preachers had come to see the sanctuary as a schoolroom and the sermon as a lecture – and in place of this I explored the idea of the preacher as poet, bard or troubadour (French *trouvère*). I wrote:

> *Consider again the content of the songs of the bards and trouvères: graphic and gripping images of life on a higher level than dull mediocrity and eminently forgettable harmlessness ....*
>
> ('Excited to Speak, Exciting to Hear', p.111)

I am in no doubt that the *cappellanus* guarding reminders of the sublime was both listener *and* raconteur par excellence. Also that it would have been said of him by the thousands who came his way, "The common people heard him gladly" – as was evidently said of Jesus (Mark 12:37).

When I duly became *cappellanus* with the University of Melbourne I was often asked what I was trying to do. Maybe questioners expected a sophisticated theological case, or some other piece of obscurantist nonsense. If that were so, they would have been disappointed. I had my stock reply: "First, make friends. Second, earn credibility. Third, get godtalk back into the arenas of public discourse – so that people might be as interested again in the relationship between the human and the holy (sometimes I'd say 'God, humanity and the cosmos') as they are in sex and football!"

If 'chaplain' could be understood simply as one who cares for reminders of the sublime, who listens and tells stories, this could be a reasonable term for the emerging religious professional – whatever the context. In my own case, there were countless conversations with faculty, staff and students who were not religiously committed but who were keenly interested in yarning about things personal with the one guarding 'reminders of the sublime'. Those eight years as 'cappellanus' are the most memorable of my sixty-one since ordination.

In my first year as 'Ecumenical Chaplain' (or *cappellanus*), and with the urging of the Vice Chancellor, Professor David Penington, I set about making connections with senior staff and faculty. I had a set 'phone patter. After saying my name and role on the campus I would ask if we could get acquainted. A science professor inquired what I wanted to talk about. "How about the interface between godtalk and cosmology?" "Well, there's none in my view. See, I'm an atheist. How long do you want?" I told him ten to fifteen minutes, and we set the time.

An hour and a half later I stumbled out of his office with his arm around my shoulder. "Sometimes," he said, "when I meet people like you I get the feeling that I may be missing out on something." We became very good friends, and had many such discussions. He came to my farewell in the Staff Club, seized the microphone and made some generous comments about Chaplaincy. Apparently, what I was trying to do was in that case working.

'Chaplain' is a term not invested with too much pretentiousness. Perhaps we could even retrieve the Latin *cappellanus*. Silly, you say? Hardly. Our discourse is already full of foreign words and phrases. If some of us were banned from using Latin, we would have to find alternatives for *status quo, quid pro quo, persona non grata, prima donna, ipso facto, modus operandi, bona fide ... ad nauseam!*

Properly understood, 'chaplain' (*cappellanus*) does have a precision all its own! I wish it could be delivered from negative definition as '*not* parish based.' Would that it might be understood properly – rather than as some kind of sanctified social worker or passion-filled missionary hell-bent on converting the lost! Whether or not the term were retrieved in the sense I have given it, this at any rate is what I am talking about as the emerging religious professional: one at his/her ease caring for reminders of the sublime, listening and telling stories – in any company! But this *does* suggest a somewhat different model from what we have inherited!

THE EDISON-TILLICH TYPE

The time is long overdue to silence the weary old chorus of "replicate, replicate, replicate! Make more ministers for outdated roles." I concluded my book 'No Fixed Address' with implications for religious leadership. The reader will find these spelled out in that work, on pages 257-264. They are immense and daunting, and they tend to be largely ignored by those responsible for selecting, training and accrediting candidates. In my judgement, as a consequence all but the most adventurous today may find they have been programmed for failure. And so, allow me to reiterate here the outlines of what I call 'The Edison-Tillich Type'. Be prepared!

Should this expression of religious leadership begin to emerge, it will be very different from the preceding generations of clergy. We are talking of men and women who combine the *analytical skill* of a Paul Tillich with the *inventiveness* of a Thomas Edison. Whether such people are being produced and/or encouraged is open to question. It may be that the culture of the church is inhospitable to them. I hope not, but the tendency is to 'standardise' ministry by tradition, by regulation and by education.

Why do I cite Edison and Tillich, and not others? These names are not plucked out of the air. Neither are they invoked for purely rhetorical purposes. I see these two figures epitomising the kind of mentality without which the future holds little promise. They represent for me what I have come to believe about religious leadership, and which would guide me today if I could re-start my career. So, who were Edison and Tillich? Surely they were two of the most exciting figures to have lived in the 19th and 20th centuries.

> (The following comes largely from my book 'No Fixed Address', pages 259-264)

Thomas Edison (1847-1931) was born in Ohio. His parents had lived in Canada, but had fled to the US after taking part in the Canadian rebellions of 1837-38. The family moved to Michigan in 1854, when Thomas was seven. His first school teacher considered him incapable of learning, describing the boy as 'addled'. His mother had been a teacher, and decided on home schooling for him.

At twelve Thomas became a newsboy on the Grand Trunk Railway. In a corner of the baggage car he set up a small printing press, and published 'The Grand Trunk Weekly Herald' – probably the only newspaper ever printed on a moving train. He was also doing experiments with chemicals. When some potion spilled, setting the baggage car alight, the conductor threw Edison and his paraphernalia off the train.

His first steady work was in railway telegraphy. Not surprisingly, his earliest inventions were refinements of telegraphic devices. At 23 he sold his interest in some of these for what was then a fortune – $40,000. He then set up a factory in New Jersey, but decided he could not be both manufacturer and inventor. So he established a laboratory there, and hired a team of skilled assistants. Edison's reputation was such by 1878 (when he was just 31) that a bunch of New York bankers put up $300,000 for a project most scientists thought crazy – developing an electric light globe.

There is dispute about some items, but Edison's overall record of inventions is probably without parallel. Not only the electric light globe, along with the central electric power system – but the gramophone, the carbon telephone, storage batteries, the dictating machine, the duplicator and motion pictures are *all* associated with Edison! In all he was awarded 1,097 US patents. In 1881, at the peak of his activity, he applied for 141 patents; one every 2½ days! During the 42 years from 1869-1910 he averaged a patent every two weeks.

A mark of Edison's thinking was his ability to connect seemingly *unrelated* sets of information, grasp their meaning and put them to practical use. One of his greatest achievements was not an invention at all. It was his ability to develop the privately financed research organisation, and to *gather a team* of creative minds; a challenging concept indeed! This style has been the basis of much of America's technical progress, and duly in the rest of the world.

Edison never stopped being the inventor. He was still working in the laboratory at his Florida home until a few weeks before he died, aged 84. Lest anyone be tempted to say, "Yes, but that was Edison, a very rare specimen indeed; had an IQ of 145", remember that Edison himself said, "Genius is one percent inspiration and ninety-nine percent perspiration."

Extraordinary, isn't it, how those who don't *want* to get the point can change the subject! On one occasion when I told this story in the context of a seminar with adults, an old fossil (probably about my age) shirtfronted me with the angry declaration that Nikolai Tesla should be credited with invention of the light globe; moreover, that Tesla had died penniless while Edison died filthy-rich. Well, maybe, maybe not; I know there is some dispute on that. But my point about imagination and inventiveness was set to one side while he savaged Edison.

Paul Johannes Tillich (1886-1965) was born in Brandenburg, then part of Germany. This made him the same age as Karl Barth, the voice of so-called 'orthodoxy', and two years older than Rudolf Bultmann, the advocate of 'demythologising'. Tillich's father was a conservative Lutheran pastor, but his mother was more liberal in her outlook. In 1911 his doctorate was conferred by the University of Breslau, and the following year he was ordained in the Lutheran church. In World War I he was a chaplain with the German military, serving at the battlefront. His close friend, the psychotherapist Rollo May (1909-94) recounted a conversation with Tillich about the impact on him of the war:

In World War I his fellow officers were brought in on stretchers, chopped to pieces by gunfire, wounded or dead. 'That night absolutely transformed me', he used to say. 'All my friends were among these dying and dead. That night I became an existentialist.' (Rollo May. 'Paulus', p.18)

After the war Tillich taught at German universities. However, in 1933 he was sacked from his university post for his views on Hitler, and went to the US in search of work. Reinhold Niebuhr (another 'preacher's kid'!) invited him to Union Theological Seminary in New York City, where he stayed until 1955. Then it was Harvard to 1962 and finally Chicago Divinity School.

I had heard of him during my initial training (52-56), but only from 'The Courage to Be', which was in the language of depth psychology and existentialism, and not regarded as a theological work. But by the 1960s, he was being hailed in the US as the theologian of the century. His name had leapt into prominence with publication of John A.T. Robinson's 'Honest to God' (1963). This was based on the work of Dietrich Bonhoeffer, Rudolf Bultmann and Paul Tillich. Jerald Brauer, at the time Dean of Chicago Divinity School, said of him:

All his life he has been speaking to the people on the borderline of religion, people who were outside the church but leaning toward it, but now the people who are in the church, even those of us in theology, find ourselves to be also on the borderline of religion. The people who are on the borderline are growing in number everywhere. They are the people for whom Tillich's theology is really made, so Tillich now has more to say than ever.

(Gary Dorrien, 'The Making of American Liberal Theology', p.517)

That observation was made more than a half-century ago. What lay behind it? It was not so much a comment on Tillich's theology as it was a comment on Tillich the man and the way he did theology. It was also a comment on the spirit of the times, and the increasing marginalisation of organised religion. In a personal interview not long before he died, Tillich himself said:

Organised Christianity makes less and less sense to the secular world. We are now living in a mass culture, and to people formed by mass media and secular interests traditional religion has no meaning. I was a chaplain in the German army in the First World War. If I used biblical language to the soldiers, it meant nothing to them – they were about to die, and yet the Bible had nothing to say to them. I preached sermons, therefore, that never used any of the language of the Bible. They were a little mystical, a little poetical, and also had a touch of common sense, and they had an effect. I think that in the secular world churches must find a new function, they must take on new meaning.

(Correspondence from a former student of Professor Tillich)

Again, a half-century ago! So, how did Tillich 'do' theology? The short answer is 'as a cosmopolitan'. Maybe 'polymath' would be a better term. Reinhold Niebuhr (1892-1971), Dean of Union Seminary when Tillich was there, said Tillich was the most learned man he had ever met. No field of human inquiry or creativity was off limits for him. In 1952 Tillich told a friend how since going to the US he had been influenced by seminars with medicos and psychiatrists, and that he wondered why there was so little dialogue between theologians and doctors! Rollo May commented on his extraordinary facility for synthesizing information from a range of sources and added:

"Tillich will be rediscovered and revalued as the thinker who does authentically speak to human beings and their condition." ('Paulus: Reminiscences of a Friendship', p.92)

Tillich was a philosopher, and much of his language reflected the existentialists, who believed that human beings had to figure out their own understanding of life's meaning. His roots went back to Schelling, Kierkegaard and Heidegger. In The Courage To Be he showed also how he was affected also by figures like Albert Camus, Franz Kafka, Arthur Miller, Tennessee Williams et al. Also, the fine arts presented a rich mine of understanding the human condition. Tillich believed that if we were to understand the spiritual temper of any culture, we should look at its art. Rollo May frequented innumerable art shows with Paul and Hannah Tillich, and over coffee afterwards they would bare their souls.

There are two specific principles that explain Tillich's theological method. One is what he called **the Protestant Principle**. By this he meant a fundamental attitude which refuses to accept any relative authority as an absolute authority. He believed that the Protestant Principle was not only the attitude that empowered the reformers to break with the papal system; it was also the principle by which the prophets of Israel challenged their own institutions. In addition, it was the principle by which biblical critics rejected the notion of an infallible book that one could not question or refute.

The Protestant Principle meant that attributing any kind of absoluteness to a theologian or a theological proposition must be challenged. To be specific, I find it extraordinary that anyone should think Karl Barth, who died in 1968 (or Tillich himself) should never have had another thought if he were still with us! The very idea is absurd.

Barth, of course, was able to laugh at his own work as a theologian, recognising that every theology is a human endeavour with all the limitations and need for continuous revision this implies. He said that when he got to heaven, he would want to have a long conversation about theological method with Friedrich Schleiermacher – say, for a couple of centuries! He imagined the angels laughing when they saw old Karl pushing his cartload of 'Church Dogmatics!'

Tillich's second axiom was **the Principle of Correlation**. His theology had two parts: the questioning, articulated by Tillich the existential philosopher and the answering, articulated by Tillich the theologian. It was his belief that philosophy helped identify and fine tune the fundamental human questions, and that the proper duty of the theologian was to draw on all the resources at his/her disposal to fashion answers to these questions.

Rollo May notes that Tillich's reputation as teacher came essentially via lectures that were always concerned with the great issues of life and death. (Rollo May. Paulus, p.114) When I taught preaching in the theological school (1977-1986), I simplified this Tillichian axiom by saying to students "Scratch where they itch!"

Now, to wrap this up! The 'creative thinking' specialist Michael Michalko, asks what it was that marked the thinking strategies of figures like Einstein, da Vinci, Darwin, Galileo, Mozart and Edison. (He could have added Tillich!) He says we cannot explain their genius simply by reference to IQ. He says some 'run of the mill' physicists have had IQs much higher than the Nobel Prize winner Richard Feynman, for example – who was widely acclaimed for his extraordinary genius, and yet had an IQ that Michalko says was a 'merely respectable' 122. He contends that a man or woman can be far more creative than he/she can be intelligent, or far more intelligent than he/she can be creative; creativity and intelligence are not synonymous. What distinguishes Michalko's creative people is the way they think:

> Typically, we think **reproductively** – that is, on the basis of similar problems encountered in the past. When confronted with problems, we fixate on something in our past that has worked before. We ask, 'What have I been taught in life, education or work on how to solve this problem?' Then we analytically select the most promising approach based on past experiences, excluding all other approaches, and work within a clearly defined direction toward the solution of the problem. Because of the soundness of the steps based on past experiences, we become arrogantly certain of the correctness of our conclusion.
>
> In contrast, geniuses think **productively, not reproductively.** When confronted with a problem, they ask, 'How many different ways can I look at it?' 'How can I rethink the way I see it?' and 'How many different ways can I solve it?' instead of 'What have I been taught by someone else on how to solve this?'
>
> (Michael Michalko, 'The Secrets of Creative Genius', p.2)

England's Sir Ken Robinson is a leader in the development of creativity, innovation and human resources in education and in business. His contention is that education not only fails to encourage creativity, but effectively suppresses it. He defines creativity as "the process of having original ideas that have value." This is a step on from imagination. Robinson emphasises that to be creative means putting one's imagination to work; also that one must be ready to take the risk of being wrong. If we are afraid of being wrong, we are unlikely to be creative. What might be the implications of this in theological education?

The Edison-Tillich type for religious leadership is as much about personality as it is of education; probably more so. Nonetheless, it does imply educational groundwork and ongoing education of a high order for men and women with what I would call 'flair' – or instinctive discernment. We can provide education; I doubt we can generate 'flair' ex nihilo. My own view is that we need to be more attentive to selecting and equipping men and women with recognisable 'flair'. They may have love and faith in abundance, but we should be wary where they have become conventional, unimaginative, habit-bound and risk-averse. We have tended to prefer these, thus perpetuating a doomed system.

If there is a future for a new, emerging church other than extinction in the foreseeable future, this will be partly because some men and women will be able to command respect for their scholarly competence, and equally to inspire experiment and risk by their elan; their ardour or enthusiasm. There could be a place for individuals like this working with communities of faith, or even 'wandering abroad' like the Quaker mystic George Fox (1624-1691) who had no formal education but a rich and enriching spirituality to sustain him and share with others. But perhaps men and women like this are a dying breed. Time will tell.

CHAPTER 9

WILL WE HAVE ANY RECRUITS?

In 1967 (admittedly a long time ago!) the late Joseph Wesley Mathews (1911-1977) was Dean of the Chicago Ecumenical Institute, an avant-garde agency of social reconstruction. He was in Australia and had invited me to join the faculty of the Institute. Then he said, almost as an afterthought, "Maybe I should tell you that where we are in Chicago it's ninety-eight percent black, and your kids will get beaten up on the way home from school most days." I thanked him for his confidence in me, and his concern for my children, and declined the invitation. Remember, that was 1967.

In that same conversation Dean Mathews had been caustic about those who ridiculed full-time church vocations. "Any young man," he said, "who dismisses the local congregation doesn't know what it means to be a revolutionary!" He went on (and this dates the observation), "The communist party would give its right arm for a cigar box with a steeple at every crossroad and corner, where people were already meeting weekly."

In other words, Mathews was asking where else does one find, faithfully gathered every week, a captive audience asking (albeit tongue in cheek) what they might do to bend history a little. 'Bending history' was a favourite expression of Dean Mathews.

In 1971 I quoted this conversation to an Adelaide friend, a well-known lawyer and product of our big Congregational youth movement in the fifties and sixties. He said, "That may once have been true, John, but all the young men and women with a fire in the belly have left the church." Even then, more than four decades ago, he and I were aware that many whose worldview and social conscience had been shaped in the church had gone off and joined some other organization they saw as more 'front line'.

Only since then have we begun to look seriously at the absence of young men and young women offering for ordination. To my knowledge, few have yet attempted to put their finger on reasons for this. Wearing my 'sociologist hat', which I still don now and then, I reject any simple, single-cause explanation for anything. There is always a whole bundle of factors at work, which exercise a cumulative effect to bring about something like this.

So, are there any young people with a fire in the belly (about anything)? Well, yes, definitely so. I have seen plenty on the steps of the Victorian State Library, demonstrating over Australia's policies vis-à-vis asylum seekers. I have wondered how many in this crowd had a churchy background or were still in it, and how many had quit on organised religion. Do we have any of those rebels, stirrers, hell-raisers, passionate young people in our congregations like those of fifty years ago? I want to be told they are there, but I fear they may die of cold. After all, there's warmth as well as strength in numbers, but the lonely battler can freeze.

And if we do have them, do they see full-time church vocations as a viable option? Or are they like some of those we were losing as far back as the 1960s and 70s – who were looking for opportunities nearer the 'front line'? In fact, are there more attractive options these days for young persons passionate about fixing up the world?

I began theological education at twenty and was ordained at twenty-five. If I were twenty again, would I do it today? The short answer is, "I would like to think so, but I cannot be sure." That is because there is a whole bunch of factors which were not part of the equation back then. I think I would be more wary of it than I was then. At least ten disincentives are present today; fifty years ago they were not. I want to list these, and then in the second section of this chapter set down some factors that could impel me toward ordained ministry if I were twenty-ish today.

But first ...

TEN DISINCENTIVES

1. Would I fancy being a geriatric social worker? Face it: there are some congregations where at least half of the faithful could be my grandparents if I were in my twenties. Unless I had a great fondness for older people, this could be rather daunting.

2. Would I manage the stress that is evidently part of the job? We hear about it all the time: freak-out, burn-out, wipe-out, break-down, drop-out. The casualty rate suggests that there is a lot of unhappiness in the profession. Do I want to put myself through that?

3. How about some of the high-powered laity who are just plain smarter and better educated than I am? Fifty years ago, clergy often had the advantage of a longer education than many of their people; they were less likely to be threatened by too many pewsitters having a 'weight advantage' in those terms.

4. Who presents an exciting role model, anymore? Again, fifty years ago there were figures in the ordained ministry who were almost legends for their oratory, their ability to rouse up a crowd, their campaigning for this and that, their unabashed public utterances for God and goodness; the Reinhold Niebuhrs, Alan Walkers, Gordon Powells et al.

5. The culture is so 'disconfirming' these days. A journo friend tells me what I already know, and hate being told: that the public image of organised religion is quite awful. She says we need a good 'PR' agency. As recently as twenty years ago, even those who did not go to church were nonetheless glad that we had churches; these were symbols of security on the cultural landscape – rather like the police, fire and ambulance services. It was good to have them, even if we rarely resorted to them. But these days the culture is downright dismissive of us.

6. Would the church really want me? In the early days of the Uniting Church in Australia, we congratulated ourselves on the number of 'mature' candidates; average age at ordination early to mid thirties. "Great stuff! These people brought a wealth of experience in 'the real world', faith refined in the blast furnace of secularism, emotional maturity, blah, blah." Were we delivering another message without really trying? That is, were we discouraging younger applicants? We were; I know it. Younger ones were often headed off.

7. Where are the theological college teaching personnel in all this? Are they high profile in church and community? How many of our pewsitters could name them? Could claim to have met them? Could claim to know them well? See them as exciting, scholarly and entertaining figures one would rather like to emulate? Or are they largely invisible, unknown, faceless individuals these days?

8. And what about the candidates in our colleges? Are the present crop 'stirrers' or are they mostly docile? Nothing intended by that. I simply do not know. It used to be that candidates who were readying themselves for ministry were first choices for camp leaders, study leaders at big conferences, and hence widely seen and known around the countryside.

9. Then there is the so-called 'shaking of the foundations'. Not a new expression at all, but a much bigger issue today than fifty years ago. The plain fact is that the old theological edifice which once stood impermeable to threat is crumbling, and everybody knows it. What is the message that I am to take with me if I am ordained?

10. Finally, will there be a church to hire me, or are the prognostications of doom about to come true? I am not sure I want to be part of something that is about to wither and die.

There are other factors to which the reader could doubtless draw my attention. Not least among them is the effect for married candidates on spouse and children – especially when the spouse did not marry a minister!

But on the other side of the equation, are there factors that might push me or others towards thinking about ordained ministry? I think there probably are. However, caution needs to be exercised in encouraging/urging/persuading them to offer. Indeed, time was when one might hear this warning …

"Stay out of it if you possibly can. Don't think about it unless you feel absolutely compelled – as if by some irresistible force!" Such was the counsel often given by older clergy to young men (as they generally were back then) considering the ministry. Behind it was the awareness that one should have a powerful sense of 'call' if he was to be sustained through a demanding and difficult profession. It was too great a risk altogether if one simply 'liked people', 'loved God' or thought it would be 'interesting work' (although these are important too).

In the first part of this chapter I listed a number of disincentives that have come into the picture since my generation offered themselves to their churches. I cannot say with any confidence what I would do today if I were twenty-ish; I would have grown up in a very different world, and been the beneficiary of a very different kind of education. Not least, my education would have taught me to question all so-called 'authorities', to think for myself, to challenge hitherto unquestioned ways of doing things. But I can say what could quite possibly push me today into a religious vocation.

TEN INCENTIVES

1. Foremost would be this sense of being 'dragged' or 'driven' into it by Something outside myself. It would be a kind of compulsion that all the contrary arguments in the world could not negate; something inexplicable, ineffable. Naturally, it would be related to ...

2. A faith or 'worldview' that had germinated within me, survived the drought and earthquake and storm and fire, and borne fruit that I wanted to share around with the parched and hungry. Ministry is in the first instance all about *sharing one's own faith*; otherwise it is just memorised empty phrases. Now, these first two 'push factors' are not the whole story. There may have been in my case, and often are, a number of other factors. For instance ...

3. The significance of inspirational men and women cannot be discounted. The Epistle to the Hebrews recognises this, with its catalogue in Chapter 11 of heroes and heroines whose life and example put fire in the belly. Most of those I know who have offered for the ministry can name a man or woman who has been a role model and inspiration to them.

4. It may be that this 'role model' or another person has put the finger on one. We have too long thought candidates for ministry should be principally self-selected – out of their private conversations with God. I understand that there used to be a tradition in the Church of Scotland whereby the Elders (daunting old blokes, they were) would say to a young chap, "Have ye ever tho't aboot the ministry, laddie?"

5. The fact that some have offered themselves after a period of private study with Melbourne's former UFT (United Faculty of Theology) or similar consortium prompts me to say that there are two other factors that could galvanise somebody. I rather hope that my friends who teach read this! One would be a 'blockbuster' course that for sheer excitement appealed to inquiring younger adults, perhaps taking it as part of their university degree; e,g, "Where the atheists have got it right."

6. Another would be a charismatic crowd-puller, who created his/her own audience of potential candidates for a religious vocation. I remember when men and women went to Harvard Divinity School just to be near Krister Stendahl, Harvey Cox or Paul Tillich, such was the charisma of these scholars. Sir John Polkinghorne, renowned physicist and theologian, would draw a crowd with a course on "Religion and Science Meet". While on this, what chance would there be for Year XII students from church schools to take such a course?

7. The challenge to help in the refashioning of faith talk and the renewing of a faith community would be a powerful driving factor today for me. It is what has helped to keep me in the professional ministry and making a nuisance of myself. If I were twenty-ish, it could well be one of those factors that pointed me toward seeking ordination.

8. I cannot dismiss the significance of a 'network'. A person is often prompted to think about vocational choices

by the sort of company he/she keeps. If you belong to a bunch of young stirrers with an urge to fix up the world, that also can be the incentive that helps focus your thoughts about the ministry. Provided you 'pay the rent' (do more or less what is expected), getting paid and housed to make a nuisance of yourself is quite some opportunity.

9. Real, down-to-earth 'love of people' may well push you into it. It may be one of the best reasons. I have quoted in ordination and induction sermons this story from the late William Sloane Coffin (1924-2006), one time Chaplain at Yale and later senior minister at New York's Riverside Church. It concerned the pastor with a southern 'bible belt' congregation who was in big trouble for his social activism. They summoned him before the board. His arch foe kicked off discussion. "You'all think ah plan to push for the pastor's resignation. Let me tell you'all one thang. When mah wife was dyin' he held her hand. When she died, he held mah hand. An' dammit, he stays!" Bill Coffin's inference from this was, "If you really and truly care about them, you can get away with a lot."

10. One last thought: an 'Open Day' at a theological college/seminary, where some of the surviving hell-raisers and stirrers and trouble-makers in one's church could talk about their ministries might just be what I needed to tune into the whispers of the Spirit.

CHAPTER 10

WHAT SHALL WE DO WITH THEM?

In Chapter 8, under 'The Tyranny of Tradition' I recounted the tale of my abortive efforts to bring about a serious review of education for ministry – albeit employing a somewhat fanciful exercise. Before advancing here a set of proposals for an alternative approach to theological education, a little 'parable', written very much tongue-in-cheek. It could be called ...

THE NATIONAL ACADEMY OF SPIN

To restore the flagging fortunes of Australian slow bowling, we propose to establish The National Academy of Spin, to raise up and equip a new generation of highly competent spin bowlers – able to mesmerise any opposition with their ingenuity. There will be a three year program built around a number of key ingredients. These will include

- Mastering the glossary of technical terms in spin bowling, such as 'doosra', 'flipper', 'googly', 'wrong-un', 'zooter' and so on. Short essays and an oral examination will assess candidates' mastery of these terms.

- Secondly, candidates will study the aerodynamics of drift, trajectory and flight, and the surface dynamics of rotation, bounce and deviation, and will be able to depict these with precise geometrical drawings.
- Third, the history of spin bowling from the 19th century will be complemented by reading the works of Richie Benaud, Jim Laker (England), Lance Gibbs (West Indies), Bishan Bedi (India) and other famous apostles of spin.
- Finally, there will also be several units on balls: the anatomy of a cricket ball, the secrets of roughing up a ball without *actually* cheating, the best uses of spit and so on.
- If candidates are found to need help with rhetoric, there will be special demonstrations of sledging offered by the renowned Ian Chappell and others.

These subjects will occupy students in the first two years of the course. In the third year they will be introduced to the practice nets, and will have several sessions under the watchful eye of Shane Warne. This will measure their understanding and internalising of the theoretical preparation. At the close of the third year, on satisfactory completion of the program, they will be issued with a certificate and considered for placement with a club, this being determined by the aptitude demonstrated. Failure in any of the academic work could be expected to delay their praxis in the nets and naturally their placements.

We believe that the weakness of Australia's spin attack is due to deficiencies in historical, doctrinal and theoretical knowledge of spin bowling, and that this course will turn around the fortunes of Australian cricket.

ASSESSING THIS IDEA!

Perhaps the foregoing would be better titled an 'allegory' rather than a parable, for it sets out to expose the idiocy of thinking spin bowlers are produced in a heavily academic environment. It seems to me that unless a man (or woman) has the basic instinct and gift for spin bowling before entering the National Academy of Spin, he/she may well be demitted with a certificate but little or no practical competence.

I have often been asked by those responsible for selecting, assessing and admitting applicants for the ordained ministry, "What should we be looking for?" My answer is almost invariably the same. "First, if this person were flung tomorrow into a parish where a level crossing smash has killed an entire family known and loved in the district, would he/she know how to care for all the devastated people?"

"And secondly, on the box Sunday by Sunday, could he/she tell a story that put a song in the heart and a spring in the step of the hearers? If the answer to either or both of those questions is 'no' or 'not sure', be very cautious!"

It seems to me that, if these abilities are not *already* present in an applicant, they are very unlikely to be in him/her after three or more years of academic training. He/she will emerge unsuited to the work of ministry but now *deluded* by having a certificate of studies passed. I have seen the evidence for this too many times.

To put my position as clearly as possible, I believe we have reached the time when the academic model should be running in parallel with, if not being *replaced* by the apprenticeship model. The former has been shown with far too many candidates to be manifestly ineffectual, but to my knowledge has never seriously been reviewed.

The concept of supervised field education was introduced to help deal with this, of course, but the time assigned to it alongside that required for academic work inevitably limited the learning outcomes. If the model of apprenticeship (from the French for 'learn') is to be effective, there has to be

- a substantial component of working – actually practicing with the tools of trade, that is
- closely tutored, supervised, encouraged and critiqued by a master craftsperson, and
- complemented with regular classroom tuition in the theoretical and technical aspects of the role.

This model of equipment for religious vocations has a sturdy history, especially in Methodism. So-called 'supervised field education' has been a modest concession to this, but has had limited effectiveness, for at least three reasons; these would have been:

- the small amount of time given to actual practice – seldom more than 300 hours in any given year, and generally less
- the varied competence of 'supervisors' – who may not be highly proficient, nor expert in sharing what skills they have
- the difficulty integrating classroom theory with coalface practice; links have often been obscure

A similar approach, not unfamiliar to modern-day religious professionals, is commonly referred to as 'Clinical Pastoral Education' (CPE for short). Designed to teach pastoral care to clergy and others, and as the major route to hospital or hospice chaplaincy, this had its origins early last century. Richard Cabot (1868-1939), a distinguished medico and adjunct professor at Harvard Divinity School, urged that candidates preparing for ordained ministry should receive clinical training similar to that which was undertaken by medical students. So began 'CPE'. This intensive learning experience has been rated by many theological graduates the most valuable ingredient in their preparation for ministry! So to the apprentice model ...

HOW WOULD IT WORK IN PRACTICE?

Quite obviously this involves a change in the ratio between classroom time and coalface time. Academically-inclined shapers of education for ministry can be expected to protest heartily. Certainly, if they read on in this chapter they will be uneasy about the future of their jobs. Perhaps that would apply also those 'crafts-persons' who are challenged by the theological school to take on apprentices! This is no mean assignment, and even if they feel up to it, not all men and women in placements would be good teachers.

The concept obliges us to return to that hypothetical I ran past colleagues in the late 70s. It was designed to focus the questions "What are the irreducible minima of ministry as we understand it?" and "What are the irreducible minima of personal and professional equipment needed?" In Chapter 10 we looked at the possibility of recovering the word 'chaplain', as one who guards reminders of the sublime, who listens to the pilgrims and who tells stories.

In the preceding chapter we had proposed nine features of 'Evolving Christianity'. To save you turning back, here they are again, below (abbreviated) – as the major themes in any education for ministry. As essay topics, each would begin:

Discuss this issue as coherently and compellingly as you can, in 3,000 words, drawing freely from your 'faith' resources (scripture, theology, tradition) and from such other resources as throw light on it.

Then would follow one of the topics that were listed as pillars of 'Evolving Christianity'.

1. It will affirm the reality of that Mystery for convenience called 'GOD', or by Jews 'Hashem' (the name), without endeavouring to contain it in doctrine or dogma
2. It will affirm the centrality of Jesus

3. It will evoke and energise humanity's native disposition toward pro-social behaviour.
4. It will provide criteria for social critique, and energise the pursuit of just and responsible society
5. It will embrace the role for humanity as custodian and carer of the planet
6. It will hold before humanity, and seek to embody in its 'followers', the dream of a functional planetary community
7. It will be the warrant for a full appreciation of the body
8. It will strive to support fruitful integration of all intellectual disciplines
9. It will promote and inform the 'journey inward'
10. It will find ways, intellectually and aesthetically worthy, for collective celebration of the foregoing.

The expectation would be that a candidate write three essays per year (i.e. 9,000 words) for three years. In addition, he/she would write and present for peer critique a sermon/homily/address on each of the eight 'existential questions' in Chapter 3, The Forbidding Future. Turn back to see what these were. Also, he/she would attend several intensives per year; e.g. Greek, Hebrew, Music, Art, Story-telling &c.

This period of 'apprenticeship' could be in one placement or several, with one or more 'supervising crafts-persons'. Details such as these are for determining by those who are ready to take up the alternative concept and work on it. I will take some persuading that it is either unworkable or unfruitful, or both!

IS THIS REALLY FANTASYLAND?

The short answer is that Western churches have been living seriously in denial for half a century, refusing to face facts and obstructing almost every effort that has been made to look honestly to the future of organised religion, and its professional functionaries. It therefore seems likely that the substance of this chapter will be either considered on its merits or, more probably, dismissed out-of-hand as was my 'hypothetical' in the 1970s – because the premises in Parts I and II are rejected.

Therefore, to pick up this idea of a very different model of religious leadership, and of equipment for it, calls for quite some boldness. It involves not only grasping something that is new, but *putting down* as obsolete much that has been considered authored in heaven. It could mean putting an end to the existing 'degree' requirements and programs, and severing links with the examining and conferring bodies. I warmly invite serious dialogue on these matters!

Of course, it may be referred to a working group – or even filed 'for attention', never to be seen again. Christopher Geraghty, one time Catholic priest and retired Sydney judge, writes of his own tradition that Rome could be 'excruciatingly slow'. He says:

> *I had heard that when the recent German Pope arrived in Rome, he was horrified when he saw the pile of unanswered letters which had accumulated over the centuries. He immediately imported a team of Germanic efficiency experts to clear the backlog. Under his orders they worked day and night for months, gradually reducing the heap, opening mouldy envelopes and doing their best to deal with the many complaints. After many months they came to the bottom of the stack, picked up the last tattered envelope, opened it with great care and found St Paul's* **Second** *Letter to the Romans! (my emphasis)*
>
> (Geraghty, Christopher. 'Dancing with the Devil', p.260)

CODA

This is not really a conclusion – if the reader is hoping for a couple of pages that will pull everything together. It is more in the nature of a 'confession'. Truth to tell, I began writing 'Two Elephants' several years ago, exasperated as I was at the time with what I considered the studied avoidance of truth in most churches, my own included. The two major issues were the future of organised religion in Western societies and specifically in Australia, and the future of the 'religious professional'.

'Two Elephants' duly took shape, more or less in the present form. Some of the material has been 'road-tested' via adult learning programs around Australia and in New Zealand, where it has commonly met with affirming nods and noises; much of it apparently has reflected the way many were thinking, although they may not have said it publicly or expressly.

But I lost heart for a book, and put the project aside. There were several reasons, but two in particular. One is that the market for books on religious topics has been in decline; it never was booming in Australia, and this cannot be expected now. My other principal reason for stepping back from 'Two Elephants' is that I believed the countervailing forces would win; in other words, few if any would take much notice of what I was saying. If I were lucky, some of the material would provoke spirited responses; more likely, it would be simply ignored, which is the common weapon of traditionalism.

If it can be said that I am arguing a 'thesis' in 'Two Elephants', it would be this: *the results of any investigation are conditional on the questions that are asked.* Pursuant to this, I have a draft in my computer (never published) provisionally titled "Asking Wrong Questions, Getting Wrong Answers, About Religious Leadership".

Prior to that, of course, are the questions we should be asking about the future of churches as we have known them. This was the focus of my doctoral research, begun informally in 1967 and duly published in 'A Matter of Death and Life' (1986). Driven by sociological method rather than by unquestioned theological presumptions, I naturally arrived at conclusions not popular among defenders of the faith.

My position has not changed: I will continue to argue that attempts to revive organised religion fail to ask the proper questions. This also means that the related subject of a future for the religious professional is similarly skewed – because the 'right' questions are not being asked. Accordingly, *Two Elephants* has addressed at some length the definition problem – "What exactly *is* religion?" alongside the motivations – "What are the drivers of religiousness? It has also looked at the role(s) of so-called 'religious professionals'. Do these have a future – and if so, in what terms? I should like the last word to come from Keith Ward, former Regius Professor of Divinity at Oxford and doughty opponent of the atheist Richard Dawkins:

> *I am, by nature and conviction, an Idealist philosopher, somebody who believes in the supremacy of Spirit or Mind, and who thinks that the material universe is an expression or creation of a Supreme Mind. I see religions as very ambiguous but probably necessary ways of giving*

humans some awareness of this Supreme Mind. I am a Christian, and became a priest of the Church of England in 1972. But I have an interest in the many diverse ways in which humans have sought spiritual truth, and in trying to understand what these various paths may have to teach.

I think the main task for religious believers today is to ensure that their beliefs are conducive to human flourishing and, so far as possible, to the flourishing of all sentient beings; to relate ancient religious beliefs to the modern scientific world view; and to see their own faith in a truly global context.

(Keith Ward Web site <https://www.keithward.org.uk/about/>)

BIBLIOGRAPHY

Armstrong, Karen. *A History of God*. New York: Ballantyne Books, 1993.
Armstrong, Karen. *The Great Transformation. The Beginning of our Religious Traditions*. New York, Toronto: Alfred A Knopf, 2006.
Armstrong, Karen. *The Case for God*. New York, Toronto: Alfred A. Knopf, 2009.
Arouet, François-Marie (pen name Voltaire) Address *"On Toleration: In Connection with the Death of Jean Calas"*, 1763.
Barrett, William. *Irrational Man: A Study in Existential Philosophy*. London: Heinemann, 1961.
Bass, Diana Butler. *Christianity After Religion: The End of Church and the Birth of a New Spiritual Awakening*. New York, NY: Harper Collins, 2012.
Blaikie, Norman. *The Plight of the Australian Clergy: to Convert, Care or Challenge?* St Lucia, Q.: University of Queensland Press, 1979.
Bodycomb, John. *Quo Vadis, Ecclesia?* Melbourne: Unpublished doctoral thesis, 1984.
Bodycomb, John. *A Matter of Death and Life: The Future of Australia's Churches*. Melbourne: Joint Board of Christian Education, 1986.
Bodycomb, John. *On Whom Hands Are Laid: Listening to the Laity and Looking to the Future*. Melbourne. Unpublished Report to Uniting Church Victoria 1998.
Bodycomb, John. *Excited to Speak, Exciting to Hear: The Art of Preaching*. Adelaide: Openbook Publishers, 2003.
Bodycomb, John. *No Fixed Address: Faith as Journey* Melbourne: Spectrum Publishing, 2010.

Bodycomb, John. *Why RELPROS Unravel.* Unpublished address, available on request, 2016.

Bodycomb, John. *One Man's Assessment of Progressive Christianity.* Unpublished paper, available on request, 2018.

Borg, Marcus. *The Heart of Christianity. Rediscovering a Life of Faith.* San Francisco: Harper Collins, 2004.

Bouma, Gary, and Anna Halafoff. *Australia's Changing Religious Profile: Views from the 2016 Census.* JASR. Sheffield: Equinox Publishing.

Bruce, Steve. *Secular Beats Spiritual. The Westernization of the Easternization of the West.* Oxford: Oxford University Press, 2017.

Cameron, Anson. *"For god's sakes ..."*, Melbourne AGE 30.3.13.

Clynes, Manfred. *Sentics. The Touch of the Emotions.* Garden City, NY: Anchor Press/Doubleday, 1978.

Cox, Harvey. *The Future of Faith.* New York, NY: Harper Collins Publishers, 2009.

Crotty, Robert. *Three Revolutions: Three Drastic Changes in Interpreting the Bible.* Hindmarsh, South Aust: Australian Theological Forum. 2012.

Davies, Paul. *The Cosmic Blueprint.* London: Unwin Hyman Limited, 1987.

Dempsey, Kenneth. *Conflict and Decline. Ministers and Laymen in an Australian country town.* Melbourne: Methuen Australia, 1983.

Dorrien, Gary. *The Making of American Liberal Theology: Idealism, Realism & Modernity.* Louisville & London: Westminster Press 2003.

Durkheim, Emile. *The Rules of Sociological Method* (translation) New York: The Free Press, 1982.

Durkheim, Emile. *The Elementary Forms of Religious Life.* (translation) New York: The Free Press, 1995.

Fosdick, H.E. *Adventurous Religion and Other Essays.* London: Student Christian Movement, 1926.

Geraghty, Christopher. *Dancing with the Devil.* Melbourne: Spectrum Publishing, 2012.

Hamilton, Clive. *Silent Invasion. China's Influence in Australia.* Melbourne: Hardie Grant Books, 2018.

Hughes, Philip J. *The Australian Clergy.* Hawthorn, Vic., Christian Research Association, 1989.

Hughes, Philip. *Charting the Faith of Australians: Thirty Years in the Christian Research Association.* Nunawading, Vic: Christian Research Association, 2016.

Hughes, Philip J. & Lachlan Fraser. *Life, Ethics and Faith in Australian Society: Facts and Figures*. Nunawading, Vic.: Christian Research Association, 2014.

Hunt, Rex A.E. & Smith, John W.H. (Eds) *Why Weren't We Told: A Handbook on 'progresive' Christianity*. Salem, OR: Polebridge Press, 2013.

Jaspers, Karl. *The Origin and Goal of History*. Abingdon UK: Routledge Revivals (translation), 2011 version.

Jud, Gerald J and Edgar W Mills. *Ex-Pastors: why men leave the parish ministry*. Philadelphia, PA: Pilgrim Press, 1970.

Jung, C.G. *Letters of C.G.Jung Vol 1 1906-1950*. Princeton, NJ: Princeton University Press, 1973.

Krippner, Stanley. *The Future of Religion*. Paper prepared for presentation at LSD: Problem Child and Wonder Drug. San Francisco, Cal., Saybrook Graduate School and Research Center, 2006.

Kuhn, Thomas. *The Structure of Scientific Revolutions*. Chicago: University of Chicago Press, 1962.

McDonald, Kathleen. *How to Meditate. A Practical Guide*. Somerville, Mass.: Wisdom Publications, 2005.

MacKenzie Brown, D. *Ultimate Concern: Tillich in Dialogue*. New York, NY: Harper & Row Publishers, 1965.

Maslow, Abraham. *A Theory of Human Motivation*. 1943. Psychological Review 50:4.

Maslow, Abraham. *Motivation and Personality*. New York, NY: Harper & Row, 1954.

Maslow, Abraham. *Toward a Psychology of Being*. New York, NY: Van Nostrand Reinhard Publishing, 1962.

May, Rollo. *Paulus: Reminiscences of a Friendship*. New York, NY, Harper & Row Publishers, 1973.

Mercadante, Linda A. *Belief without Borders: Inside the Minds of the Spiritual but not Religious*. New York, NY: Oxford University Press, 2014.

Michalko, Michael. *Cracking Creativity: The Secrets of Creative Genius*. Berkeley, Cal.: Ten speed Press, 2001.

Micklem, Nathaniel. *A Religion for Agnostics*. London: SCM Press, 1965.

Nagel, Thomas. *Mind and Cosmos. Why the Materialist Neo-Darwinian Conception of Nature is Almost Certainly False*. New York, NY: Oxford University Press, 2012.

New Zealand Hymnbook Trust. *Hope is our Song: New Hymns and Songs from Aotearoa New Zealand*. Wellington, NZ: Philip Garside Publishing Ltd, 2009.

Nisbet, Robert A. *The Social Bond. An Introduction to the Study of Society*. New York, NY: Alfred A Knopf, Inc, 1970.

Parkinson, Lorraine. *The World According to Jesus: His Blueprint for the Best Possible World*. Melbourne: Spectrum Publishing, 2011.

Peacocke, Arthur. *The Religion of a Scientist*. Zygon Journal of Religion & Science Vol.29, No.4. Dec 1994, pp.639-659.

Peacocke, Arthur, in *Science & Spirit* (discontinued bi-monthly). Washington, DC: Templeton Foundation.

Polkinghorne, John and Nicholas Beale. *Questions of Truth. Fifty-one Responses to Questions about God, Science, and Belief*. Louisville, KY: Westminster John Knox Press. 2009.

Robertson, Geoffrey. *The Case of the Pope: Vatican Accountability for Human Rights Abuse*. Penguin Australia, 2010.

Robinson, John A.T. *Honest to God*. London: SCM Press, 1963.

Smart, Ninian. *The Future of Religion*. Interview with Ninian Smart, adapted from BBC public radio series "Insight and Outlook", 1999.

Smith, Durham. *Search for Understanding: Is there a problem with Traditional Theology?* Melbourne: Mini Publishing, 2006.

Southgate, Christopher et al. *God, Humanity and the Cosmos: A Textbook in Science and Religion*. Edinburgh: T & T Clark, 1999.

Spong, John Shelby. *A New Christianity for a New World: Why Traditional Faith is Dying & How a New Faith is Being Born*. New York, NY: Harper Collins.

Spong. John Shelby. *Why Christianity must change or die*. San Francisco: Harper Collins, 1998.

Steele, Bruce. *The Organ in St Aidan's Church, North Balwyn*. North Balwyn, Vic: St Aidan's Music Society. 2000.

Stiglitz, Joseph. *Globalization and Its Discontents*. New York, NY: W.W.Norton & Co, 2002.

Stone-Davis, Férdia J. (Ed) *Music and Transcendence*. Farnham (Surrey): Ashgate, 2015.

Stotts, Herbert E. et al. *A Study of Southern California Baptist Churches 1969*. Boston, Mass: Boston University School of Theology, 1970.

Suter, Keith. *The Future of the Uniting Church in Australia. The application of Scenario Planning to the Creation of 'Futures' for the Uniting Church in Australia*. Unpublished doctoral thesis, made available privately.

Tacey, David. *The Spirituality Revolution – The Emergence of Contemporary Spirituality*. Sydney, NSW: Harper Collins Pty Ltd., 2003.

Tanner, Marcus et al. 'Forced Termination of American Clergy', Review of Religious Research 54:1, March 2012, pp.1-17.

Taussig, Hal. *A New Spiritual Home: Progressive Christianity at the Grass Roots.* Santa Rosa, Cal.: Polebridge Press, 2006.

Taylor, Charles. *A Secular Age.* Cambridge, MA: Harvard University Press, 2007.

Templeton, John Marks. *The Humble Approach: Scientists Discover God.* New York, NY: Continuum Publishing Co., 1995.

Templeton, John Marks and Kenneth Seeman Giniger (Eds). *Spiritual Evolution. Scientists Discuss Their Beliefs.* Philadelphia & London: Templeton Foundation Press, 1998.

Templeton, John. *The Quotable Sir John – on Life and Spirituality.* Philadelphia & London: Templeton Press.

Thoreau, H.D. *Essay on Resistance to Civil Government,* first published 1849. Retrieved via Internet.

Tillich, Paul. *The Shaking of the Foundations.* Penguin, 1962.

Toffler, Alvin. *Future Shock.* New York, NY: Random House, 1970.

Ward, Keith. *Pascal's Fire. Scientific Faith and Religious Understanding.* Oxford: One World. 2006.

Ward, Keith. *Why There Almost Certainly Is a God. Doubting Dawkins.* Oxford: Lion Hudson, 2008.

Ward, Keith. *The Big Questions in Science and Religion.* West Conshohocken, PA, 2008.

Ward, Keith. *More than Matter: Is there more to Life than Molecules?* Grand Rapids, MI: William B Eerdmans Publishing Company, 2011.

Ward, Keith. Web Site https://www.keithward.org.uk/about/.

Waterhouse, Eric. *The Dawn of Religion.* London: Epworth, 1936.

Webb, Val. *Like Catching Water in a Net: Human Attempts to Describe the Divine.* New York, NY, and London: Continuum International Publishing, 2007.

Webb, Val. *Still Doubting Boldly.* Lecture to Progressive Christian Network of Victoria, March 2013.

Wood, Douglas & Cheng-Khee Chee (illustrator). *Old Turtle.* New York NY: Scholastic Press, 1992.

www.ingramcontent.com/pod-product-compliance
Lightning Source LLC
Chambersburg PA
CBHW050556300426
44112CB00013B/1936